D0662260

SLEEPING BAGS
TO S'MORES

SLEEPING BAGS TO S'MORES

CAMPING BASICS

HEATHER BALOGH ROCHFORT & WILLIAM ROCHFORT

ILLUSTRATED BY LAURA FISK

Houghton Mifflin Harcourt

Boston   New York

2020

Copyright © 2020 by Heather Balogh Rochfort and William Rochfort

Illustrations by Laura Fisk copyright © 2020 by Houghton Mifflin Harcourt

All rights reserved

For information about permissions to reproduce selections from this book, write to trade.permissions@hmhco.com or to Permissions, Houghton Mifflin Harcourt Publishing Company, 3 Park Avenue, 19th Floor, New York, NY 10016.

hmhbooks.com

Library of Congress Cataloging-in-Publication Data
Names: Rochfort, Heather Balogh, author. | Rochfort, William (Backpacker Magazine editor) author. | Fisk, Laura, illustrator.
Title: Sleeping bags to s'mores : camping basics / Heather Balogh Rochfort and William Rochfort ; illustrated by Laura Fisk.
Description: Boston : Houghton Mifflin Harcourt, 2020. | Includes index.
Identifiers: LCCN 2019033948 (print) | LCCN 2019033949 (ebook) | ISBN 9780358100317 | ISBN 9780358306900 | ISBN 9780358306962 | ISBN 9780358098515 (ebook)
Subjects: LCSH: Camping. | Outdoor recreation. | Wilderness areas.
Classification: LCC GV191.7 .R64 2020 (print) | LCC GV191.7 (ebook) | DDC 796.54 – dc23
LC record available at https://lccn.loc.gov/2019033948
LC ebook record available at https://lccn.loc.gov/2019033949

Book design by Amy Sly

Printed in China

TOP 10 9 8 7 6 5 4 3 2 1

For Liliana. Always.

CONTENTS

CHAPTER ONE

PICKING THE DESTINATION

Of the two of us, Will is definitely the aggressive planner. At any given moment, he can tell you the locations and dates of the next ten to fifteen hiking trips we have planned, as well as the major international trips we'll take for the next four years. In a way, he feels the same about planning trips as George R. R. Martin feels about writing—the good ones end up being epics, but he enjoys the state of having *completed* the task much more than the act of doing it. (As for Heather? She prefers surviving the day.) But Will continues on with his type-A planning personality because it is the sole act that has taken us on hundreds of hiking trips. And even though we're nearly halfway through our lifetimes and our bodies are nearly half dead, we intend to head out on hundreds more.

If you are a first-timer, planning a trip into the wilderness can be intimidating. For clarity, you *will* make mistakes and you *will* do something like pack the wrong gear. (We can talk later about that time Will brought three extra-large sweatshirts and four gallons of water on his first backpacking trip, or that one adventure when Heather thought canned soup was the best way to cut her backpack size.) Bottom line: The biggest mistake you can make is not to go.

We are not advocating for lack of preparedness, but we are strongly endorsing the 40/70 Rule: You need at least 40 percent of the available information to make a decision, and once you get beyond 70 percent you should lean on intuition to fill in the gaps rather than postpone actually doing something (mad thanks to Colin Powell for that life advice). Start by simply focusing on your destination selection. Decide on one of the types of trips outlined here, do a reasonable amount of research on your destination, find a friend and/or unsuspecting significant other to join you, and then set the date to sleep on some dirt. If you really want to emotionally overcommit, make it Facebook official and tell everyone

else who is scrolling their phone in some corporate meeting that you are GOING CAMPING. Nothing says commitment like declaring intent on social media.

We like to break hiking trips out into three categories: day hikes, overnights, and dispersed camping. The distinctions among the three drive the destinations we are interested in as well as our gear loadout. Ergo, depending on how much time you have and how many times you want to cry because of your heavy pack weight, you may lean toward one particular style more than another.

Of course, many blur the lines among the three. For example, most civilized humans treat Colorado's iconic Four Pass Loop as a four-day backpacking trip, but there are absurdly ambitious individuals who hike/run the twenty-eight miles in a single day under the auspices of "fun." You do you.

DAY HIKES

This could be a low-key hike to a backcountry hot spring, or it could be a twenty-mile Jake-and-Elwood Mission from God. The punch line is that it is a hike you complete in a day, which means that finding a destination with a particular highlight will likely make the day more interesting. For our family, this usually means peak-bagging a Colorado fourteener (a summit with an elevation of at least 14,000 feet), although we've also made a day of tracking down champion trees in the Eastern Sierra, secret waterfalls in Montana, and the perfect whale-watching outcropping on the Channel Islands.

The real perk here is the lightweight backpack. Unfettered by the trappings of overnight accommodations, your pack weight might be only around ten pounds, making it much easier to cover unholy distances or scramble up a talus field. Or you can be a real mensch and secretly stash a six-pack of summit beers. Even if you don't imbibe, you will be an instant legend when you deliver a life-changing libation after a grueling high-altitude climb. Whatever you carry, don't be a rube and skimp on the Ten Essentials (which we reveal on page 32) because you want to save a few ounces. Even if you don't end up needing the gear, you could save someone else's tail on the trail.

A further word on safety: Anecdotally, day hikers are the most likely to get stuck in an unintentionally undesirable situation. When you're backpacking, you have your entire world on your shoulders, and in most circumstances, you can safely pitch a tent if the weather takes a nasty turn. With a lightweight daypack, you are either going to have to construct a shelter out of the flimsy shell jacket and granola bar from the bottom of your pack, or optimistically hope Les Stroud is sharing your trail today. It can happen fast: On a trip to the Ansel Adams Wilderness several years back, one of our friends went for a quick hike in running shoes, a T-shirt, and the kind of shorts that reveal a blinding amount of upper man thigh. He was an experienced backcountry hiker as well as accomplished marathoner, yet fifteen minutes after departing camp he slipped while traversing a snowfield, and without an ice axe to arrest, he slid hundreds of feet down to the lake below. Although he left camp on a 75-degree midsummer day, temps were in the mid-40s when he limped the several miles back to camp twelve hours later. Aside from a gruesome ice rash (although we all agreed it was karma for wearing the short shorts) and moderately wounded pride, he was lucky to be no worse for wear.

OVERNIGHTS

There are entire tomes dedicated to the fine art of selecting overnight backpacking locations, so we shall not endeavor to condense them to a few hundred words here. However, we would offer some valuable lessons learned.

Start with attainable mileage goals. If you get to camp sooner than expected, congrats! Go fishing, or enjoy your book or the unbridled company of friends who are temporarily released from the tyranny of their cellular devices.

We are #blessed to live in one of the most geographically gifted countries in the world. We've backpacked in Tasmania, Jordan, New Zealand,

South Africa, Iceland, and others, and if we were told we could hike only in one country for the balance of our coexistence, we would choose the American West and never look back. Once you get a few local trips under your belt, pick an iconic American destination and book it. Also, take the time to dig deeper than the first page of Google results. Yes, everyone should visit the Canyonlands if they can, but have you ever heard of Red Break in Escalante National Monument? Or, in addition to Yosemite's Half Dome, check out Second Lake in the Palisades. (It is the best bang-for-buck overnight in existence, in our humble opinions.)

If the forecast looks sketchy, don't be afraid to bail. Every year people perish thanks to lightning strikes, flash floods, and a host of other avoidable natural causes. Yes, it is extremely difficult to pull the plug on the Zion trip you've been planning for months, but that is significantly better than asking a loved one to make the decision on whether to pull your plug after search-and-rescue (SAR) scrapes you from the bottom of a slot canyon without a pulse. The summits will be here tomorrow—make sure you are too.

DISPERSED CAMPING

This is where we indulge. In our chronologically advanced state, we've developed a new appreciation for dispersed camping, which is a particular variety of car camping. Previously, Will believed car camping meant you were stuffed into an organized campground with loud snorers, cranky generators, and a peculiar number of white windowless vans, but that is only for those unwilling to do a little homework. (Thankfully, Heather showed him the error of his ways.) Certain wilderness areas such as National Forest and BLM land (that's the Bureau of Land Management) allow dispersed camping at-large or in designated sites, and it is usually free. One of our favorite spots is along the Laramie River in northern Colorado's Arapahoe National Forest. We pulled up in late summer to a hazy, backlit campsite with our own private swimming hole and a decrepit (yet

romantic) old cabin that had misplaced its roof years before. After rigging hammocks, we kicked our feet up and swayed in the breeze, reveling in our superior intelligence that accidentally led us to the location.

Or, here is another one of our favorite plays: See if there is a national forest that abuts your favorite national park. For example, when visiting Bryce Canyon National Park, we stayed thirty minutes away in Dixie National Forest, where the camping is free and we had a private creek-side campsite to ourselves. Even though the paid campgrounds are booked in the park months in advance, we showed up in early summer and had no trouble finding a site. The added bonus: Since we were camping with our seven-month-old daughter, we didn't have neighbors giving us salty looks the next morning because of her random bouts of wailing in the middle of the night.

Take a look at the public lands near you, check the camping restrictions, and then simply pick a spot based on what looks good on a map. We've stumbled upon our favorite camping spots this way, many of which we return to year after year, and almost all of which never show up in a guidebook. And since you are car camping, you have every reasonable amenity you could possibly ask for, and then some. Bring your favorite pillow from home, your queen-size air mattress, and your full-size camping chair. Treat yo'self and pack a bottle of wine, too. Dispersed camping is an embarrassment of riches.

CHAPTER TWO

CAMPING INSIDE OR OUT

Camping comes in a variety of different strokes for different folks. Although we'd largely consider ourselves time-tested backpackers, we take great satisfaction in staying outdoors in whatever shelter suits the circumstances. We have strong emotional attachments to backcountry cabins with wood-burning stoves in the winter; in midsummer, we are happy to leave the tent at home when we feel optimistic. The point is that there is not one right way to do it. Tent or no tent, the only thing you can do wrong is to marinate at home on the couch instead of getting out and putting some nature in front of yourself.

COWBOY CAMPING

We understand why someone may be reticent to sleep sans shelter. What about unexpected weather? Will I get cold? What about *bugs and snakes?!* Urban legends tell us that most humans consume eight spiders every year, and this usually happens while sleeping in beds inside cozy, warm, and properly sealed homes. We'd argue that if you are going to ingest an arachnid, you might as well get your money's worth and sleep under the stars.

Assuming the weather cooperates, this is by far our favorite kind of camping. It brings back the romance of the American West, and it is easy to see the world in the same way as those who lived here hundreds of years before us (not to mention it affords you an extremely lightweight pack). Thanks to three ACL surgeries resulting in an octogenarian's knees, Will always hikes with trekking poles, which means we can drop a five-ounce tarp in one of our packs and always be able to rig a crisis shelter if necessary. Otherwise, save the couple of pounds of weight and cram everything you need into an oversize daypack. Stripping your shelter will help you find other ways to cut unnecessary weight (you don't really need a fresh pair of socks for each day). You will cover more ground, see more wilderness, and genuflect on the fact that Sacagawea covered double-digit miles while pregnant and carrying at least triple what you have.

If you really want to do it right, time it with a meteor shower like the Perseids in early August. Stargazing through tent mesh is like kissing your second cousin—technically allowed, but probably not what you want to be doing. This is an annual celestial event, and if you've never seen a proper meteor shower, whatever shooting stars you've seen up to this point will feel like a cheap imitation. These meteors glow greens and purples and leave streaks across the sky when they burn through the atmosphere. It is the kind of event that will reconstitute your perspective of the universe.

TENT CAMPING

We'd surmise this is what most people picture when they imagine going camping. Do not underestimate the romance of putting your entire life on your back for a weekend (or longer), heading into backcountry, and creating a temporary home wherever you end up. Even though only a thin nylon wall separates you from the elements, once you get that tent pitched, sleeping mat inflated, sleeping bag lofted up, and have cozied up next to your tentmate, you will feel like you are tucked away safely in the Shire. Several years ago, we experienced an approaching army of cumulonimbus clouds while backpacking near Zapata Lake in Colorado's Sangre de Cristo Mountains. We barely had our Hubba Hubba tent pitched in the grove before the sky opened up. It started with hail before turning to heavy rain; the storm was so close it seemed the thunder preempted the lightning, and every clap rattled the granite walls as well as our internal organs. It was exhilarating, and we would do it again in a heartbeat.

CAMPERVANS

Neither of us will ever forget the first night of our honeymoon in Canada. (No, not for that reason. Calm down!) Thanks to our Volkswagen Eurovan's maxed-out uphill speed of fifty-five miles per hour, it took us two days to drive from Denver to Alberta for ten days of autumn camping along the Icefields Parkway. We pulled into the rainy Lake O'Hara Trailhead in Yoho National Park just before sunset, popped the top, and turned on the thermostat. Will cooked dinner while Heather snuggled with our mutt on the back seat. Safely ensconced in our German incubator, we enjoyed three-cheese ravioli, a side salad, and red wine while watching the snow lilt to the forest floor on the other side of the windshield. Cheesy but true: Home was where we parked it.

From that night forward we've been strong advocates for campervan travel. As the previous story underscores, it is extremely satisfying to arrive at the trailhead in inclement weather and not futz with tent poles. Additionally, while we have slept in a nylon tent in 15-below weather in Yellowstone, we both readily concede to the perks of waking up in a climate-controlled van in subfreezing conditions. Campervans also afford a degree of spontaneity that you don't get with hotels or traditional backcountry tent camping. When we traveled to Alberta, our plan was to simply look at the map each morning and decide which trail to go hike next, and it was one of the most relaxing hiking trips either of us has ever enjoyed. If we loved a trail, we would stay an extra night. If we arrived somewhere and it looked crowded, we'd keep right on going until we found the solitude we wanted.

Additionally, campervans are the perfect way to dip your toes into hiking in cold weather with your kids. We brought our five-month-old baby girl on a campervan trip to Iceland in March, and she thought it was the greatest thing on Planet Earth. Note: She didn't care about Iceland, but *that van!* We rented a larger van than our honeymoon iteration because it featured a lofted bed. This wasn't for our daughter; rather, we needed a place to stash the ungodly amounts of baby luggage that slightly exceeded the combined weight of two adults' belongings. Will still can't justify why a tiny human necessitates that much stuff, but he only has 49 percent of the vote, so he finally quit trying.

We drove around the Snaefellsnes Peninsula for nearly a week, and it immediately became apparent just how convenient a house-on-wheels is when traveling with an infant. When she needed to breastfeed, we pulled over by Kirkjufell Mountain and opened the sliding doors on either side, and Heather sat in the sunshine with a cross breeze and a multimillion-dollar view of one of Iceland's most famous landmarks. If she needed to nap, we'd find the nearest trailhead and take turns hiking and taking photos while the other relaxed on the queen-size bed in the back of the van. As an added bonus, campervans can be a way to save some cash. We did the math in Iceland, and it was cheaper to rent the campervan and sleep on the road than book a regular passenger vehicle and stay in hotels. Pro tip: Travel to Iceland in the shoulder season, and most amenities are half price compared to the summer-season rate. You're more likely to catch northern lights anyway.

BACKCOUNTRY HUTS AND YURTS

Backcountry huts (specifically Colorado's 10th Mountain Division Huts) have completely ruined us. The luxuries afforded by solid walls and a wood-burning stove are too good to pass up, *especially* if we add winter conditions to the mix. We've watched nearly a foot of snow fall outside our glass window at Uncle Bud's Hut near Leadville, Colorado, while sipping on mulled wine and lounging in our long underwear. Perhaps even more memorable was a chilly trip to Colorado's State Forest State Park. Temps dropped to -5 degrees but we kept pouring logs into the wood-burning stove until we had a 90-degree swing between internal and external temperatures. It was lovely around dinnertime, but once we went to bed, the people sleeping on the top bunks almost perished from heat exhaustion.

The punch line is that backcountry huts can extend your season if you are not interested in camping in subfreezing temps in midwinter. We get it, and the worst part is that the kicker isn't the cold; it is the long nights. Tucking in at four-thirty p.m. and waiting for the sun to come up is an unpleasant way to spend an evening (exacerbated by loneliness if you're chilling in there by yourself). But if you can arrive at the front door of the hut or yurt just before sunset and cook dinner with your friends in a cozy cabin, we're in. Many of the structures also include kitchens, ranging from lightly kitted kitchenettes to fully stocked cook sets with acres of counter space. Elk chorizo may be the fanciest backcountry meal we've ever eaten, although we'll happily consume a giant offering of tortellini with a hearty Alfredo sauce.

Check your local offerings for backcountry accommodations for rent in your area. Extremely popular destinations like Colorado's 10th Mountain Division Huts typically book all of their weekends an entire season in advance, but lesser-known destinations such as the Opus Hut have openings until the start of the season (plus, the Opus Hut comes with a chef!).

CHAPTER THREE

WHAT TO PACK

We'll admit: We are gear junkies. Our basement is lined with perfectly arranged garment racks, shelving, and a variety of other organizational delights so that we can easily see every scintilla of our kit. It brings us great joy to know the space is also organized by the style of trip and season. Of course, this is not surprising to anyone who knew Will as a child, as he used to spend Saturdays trying to find ways to more efficiently organize his bedroom and toy closet. (Yes, Heather still teases him about this!)

We routinely take friends on their first backcountry outing, so whenever someone asks us what they should pack, we usually lead them down to our gear cellar. This year marks a decade of testing and covering gear for the outdoor industry, so at any given time, we have a number of prototypes, beta projects, and other gear that is yet to come to market. Those make great highlights as we talk about what is new for outdoor gear. But truthfully, those are just fun pieces for cocktail conversation, as the basics of hiking gear have not changed in the twenty years we've been routinely camping, especially if you are looking at starting with day hikes.

Lamentably, we cannot offer guided cellar tours to every reader. In lieu of providing a detailed schematic of our layout, we will explain what to pack in the same way we'd talk to someone if they came over for dinner. Also, the internet is rife with excellent lists of what to pack, but we'd like to add a level of "why to pack this way" that is not readily obvious.

THE TEN ESSENTIALS

No matter what trip you're going on, bring these with you. The title is relatively self-explanatory, but at the risk of being obvious, these are items essential to your survival *if* you get in over your head. We've never used all of these items on the same trip, but always use at least one of them, and we would rather not play Russian roulette and guess which one we can leave at home to save pack weight.

A note to history nerds: This is not the original Ten Essentials list published in the 1967 classic *Mountaineering: The Freedom of the Hills*. That list focused on specific items such as maps, whereas this new list focuses on a category of an item such as "navigation." The intent is the same, but know that if you get into a discussion with a salty old-school Eagle Scout, he may have some disagreement with your language.

1. *Navigation:* These are the tools that help you find your way. A GPS can be a life-saving device, and our family has successfully used an iPhone as our GPS device during a four-day paddling trip near the Everglades. That said, we still had an analog map and compass tucked in our dry bag just in case. As a personal rule, if it requires batteries, we carry backup. As with all equipment, make sure you understand how your navigation tool works before you are in the field. (Do yourself a favor and don't do something like our friend who didn't realize he needed to load the correct map into his GPS before using it.) If you are employing a map and compass, at least understand how to apply basics like declination

and triangulation. (We swear, those are real words. See chapter 9 for an explanation.)

2. *Sun Protection:* Sunburns are dumb, and generally you have no one to blame other than yourself when it happens. Not only are they painful, but you can legitimately get second-degree burns if you try to be too cool for sunscreen, especially if you are getting cooked by the reflection from water or snow. (Just ask Heather's twenty-three-year-old self after a climb up Mount Rainier's infamous glacier fried her face so severely that skin was actually peeling off in random patches.) Pack the sunscreen, and cover up as much as you can. We almost always hike in long-sleeved lightweight hoodies and hats during the summer, although Will has yet to capitulate to the dad sun sombrero.

3. *Insulation:* Don't plan for the weather you see at the trailhead; plan for the worst weather you might see that day. In Colorado, for example, this means packing a puffy jacket during midsummer mountain ascents. On more than one occasion we've seen a 40-degree swing between sunny summit temps and nasty hailstorms that show up an hour later. Even if your weather isn't that fickle, pack an extra layer just so you have something dry in case you get soaked.

4. *Illumination:* Your smartphone does not count. We'd recommend a headlamp over a flashlight, as hands-free operation is particularly handy when you are trying to climb in the dark.

5. *First-Aid Kit:* You can assemble your own or keep it simple and purchase an off-the-shelf model. Most important, don't forget to restock it when you inevitably use pieces of it on your trips. It is fairly disappointing to carry a kit and realize you never refilled the gauze and butterfly bandages while your friend is profusely bleeding, you know? Also, if you are not a backcountry health expert, consider packing a small book that describes serious injuries and how to treat them with limited supplies. We've never needed it but always found it worth the weight.

6. *Fire:* We always carry a lighter and a handful of waterproof matches. Adding firestarters like petroleum jelly-soaked cotton balls stored in a

THE →TEN←

NAVIGATION

SUN PROTECTION

¡ILLUMINATION!

INSULATION

film canister is a good idea if you are hiking in environs where fires are allowed and you could desperately need one.

7. Repair Kit and Tools: This could mean a handful of different things depending on your loadout (although we always pack a multitool with a blade), but here are a few atypical pieces we carry on nearly every trip:

a. A replacement hip belt buckle. Will was on a cross-country skiing trip out to Yosemite's Glacier Point when his buddy took a digger and smashed his buckle on a rock. (To be fair, a few inches in another direction would have required more than a few pieces of plastic to put it back together, so this truly was the best-case scenario.) Carrying all of your pack weight on your shoulders is highly undesirable, and a ninety-eight-cent featherweight piece of gear can be a lifesaver.

b. Shoestring. Sure, you could tie them together to repair it, but they weigh practically nothing, and you look like a hero when you pull them out of your pack to repair some sap's shoelaces that frayed after five years of not caring for them.

c. Tent splint. These come with most tents these days, but we always carry a spare. We've snapped several tent poles while testing gear, and a simple splint always gets us home.

8. Nutrition: Evaluate how much food you need, and then bring a little more. We make it calorie-dense and focus on nutrition over flavor; hunger is a phenomenal seasoning. If we ever get to the point when we are tapping in to our reserve meals, we likely don't care what they taste like.

9. Hydration: Bless the metric system. One liter of water weighs one kilo —how brilliant is that? Unfortunately, that also means it can be tempting to skimp on H_2O because the stupid stuff weighs so much, but it weighs less than being dead. When it is hot, carry one gallon of water per person per day. On the upside, you're incentivized to stay hydrated, since the more you drink, the less your pack weighs! Bonus tip: Keep spare iodine tablets so you can always clean some water if you get stuck in a pinch.

10. Emergency shelter: If the weather is moderately warm and dry, we will carry only a spare emergency bivy, which is essentially a sleeping bag constructed from ultra-thin, space-age heat-reflective material that keeps you warm and dry. If it is somewhere that is perpetually rainy, we will pack a spare tarp. Then we can rig a dry area with extra shoelaces (see above) and trekking poles if we are totally desperate. We haven't had to use it in a true emergency, but it has made more than one useful lunch shelter—the most noteworthy being on the banks of the Alatna River in Gates of the Arctic National Park when we tried to eat our so-dium-rich freeze-dried meals in sideways rain. (We still can't believe we paid money to go on that *vacation!*)

A final note on the Ten Essentials: These are intended to always be on your person, so leaving them at camp while you head out for a short walk doesn't count. This happens a lot: We had a friend who turned back early from a summit attempt in the Ansel Adams Wilderness and got lost on her way back to camp. Fortunately, she ran into an SAR team performing weekend training and realized she was in the entirely wrong valley to the south of our camp. She eventually made her way back home right after we returned to find her tent empty, and panicked.

Beyond the Ten Essentials, your packing will vary based on the style of trip. We categorize them as the following:

DAY HIKING

This assumes you plan on departing from and returning to the trailhead in the same day (or at least you don't plan on setting up camp). In addition to the Ten Essentials, we recommend the following for most conditions.

Daypack: This is the colloquial term for a small backpack. Since you are out only for one day and will ostensibly need fewer items than on an overnight trip, consider starting with something in the fifteen- to twen-ty-five-liter range. The smaller the pack, the harder it will be to fit in the extra stuff you don't need.

DAY HIKE ESSENTIALS

APPAREL

WATERPROOF
SHELL

SUNGLASSES

15-25 Liter
DAY PACK

EXTRA
SOCKS

SUNDRIES

FOOTWEAR

HAT and
GLOVES

Waterproof Shell: Even if it doesn't rain, most shells double as excellent windbreaks.

Extra Pair of Socks: If you sweat through one or they somehow get soaked (like maybe you slip off a log into a creek), these can change your life.

Hat and Gloves: You lose egregious amounts of heat from your head and extremities, and these few items can make an enormous difference in managing warmth.

Sundries: Bring spare contacts, inhaler, etc. if you have those sorts of needs.

Apparel: Shirt, pants, underbritches, socks, hat; we imagine you wouldn't walk out the door without these things on your body, but we feel morally obligated to list them all the same. Choose materials that dry quickly, breathe well, and fit comfortably under a pack. If you already have technical athletic apparel, it will likely work for hiking, too.

Footwear: Don't feel compelled to wear those leather Timberlands all the cool kids had in high school; we've progressed immensely since then. Since you have a slighter load than a fully packed overnight backpack, feel free to employ a lighter pair of hikers (the old-school rule of thumb says one pound on your feet is equivalent to five pounds on your back). We'd recommend procuring a pair of trail runners instead of leaning on trainers you may already have in your kit, as the latter are likely not built for the abuse on the trail, and neither are they waterproof if you need that type of weather protection.

Sunglasses: Once Will got corneal ulcers while climbing Mount Whitney, and his eyes became so sensitive to light that he had to hike down from advanced camp with his eyes closed. To be fair, the ulcers were from his contacts, but we totally got you to look, right? The point is this: Always wear quality sunglasses, *especially* when you are at altitude or on the snow. Going blind is terribly inconvenient in the backcountry, and it can happen fast.

OVERNIGHT BACKPACKING

You've come to the point where sleeping in the dirt is more appealing than *one more night* of listening to your roommate try to convince you of the importance of air-speed velocities of European swallows (or was it African swallows?). Get packing. In addition to the Ten Essentials and what is already listed on the day hiking list above, you'll want the following:

Backpack: Upgrade from the fifteen- to twenty-five-liter range to the thirty- to fifty-liter range. You are carrying your entire life on your back, and that is a beautiful thing.

Shelter: Most folks will opt for a tent because it is fun having your personal adult fort, but you can go light and choose a simple tarp if you prefer.

Sleeping Bag: Will personally has a strong affinity for sleeping bags as he has studied, researched, and written about the topic quite frequently over the years. However, we will skip the dissertation and simply say you should bring one. If you are going to have only one in your quiver, pick one in the 15-degree temp rating range.

Sleeping Pad: Getting a sleeping pad with a slightly higher R-value (the pad's ability to insulate you from the cold harsh reality of the ground on which you are sleeping) can greatly increase how warm you sleep.

Kitchen Kit: This includes a stove, fuel, cup, and utensils. If you want to go really light, you can bring only food that doesn't require heating so you can leave the stove and fuel at home. Just know that one of us will likely try to stab you with a titanium spork if you ask to borrow some hot water for your pine-needle tea.

Food: More on this in the next chapter, but here is the short version: You can bring whatever you want as long as you are willing to carry the weight. We once had a friend bring an entire cold pizza for his lunch on our winter hike in the Trinity Alps. Envy factor: all-time high.

Water filter: Iodine tablets are no way to live, no matter what our ultra-light friends say. (That taste!) Pack a filter, skip the giardia, and enjoy some fresh water straight from the source.

Apparel: Resist the urge to bring fresh clothes for every day. We know it sounds savage, but hear us out. In general, we bring two pairs of socks, one top and bottom for hiking, and one top and bottom for sleeping (since sleeping in your sweaty clothes can get you chilled in a hurry). As for extra underbritches, we'll jot that down as a personal preference.

Footwear: Bring camp shoes. Yes, it is a luxury, but it is divine. Even a super-light pair of sandals can make a world of difference at the end of a grueling day of climbing talus. Heather's luxury item is always down booties, which are essentially miniature sleeping bags for your feet. They feel as soft as marshmallows and are worth every ounce of added weight.

DISPERSED CAMPING

You essentially want the same kit as described above, but go luxe at every opportunity. Bringing a tent? Pack a ten-person chateau with a six-foot ceiling height and ample room for a disco party. Cooking dinner? Bring a cast-iron Dutch oven and make something posh on the campfire. As long as it fits in the trunk of your car, you can bring it.

Here is a final thought: There are myriad other fun toys to add to your pack; you simply need to decide if the proverbial juice is worth the squeeze. We like packing a three-ounce kit that turns a sleeping pad into a chair. Necessary? Nope, but worth it. Thanks to our combined four knee surgeries, one of us always hikes with trekking poles, too. This list is meant to be the minimum you need to safely have fun. For better or for worse, it is only the beginning.

CHAPTER FOUR

WHAT TO EAT AND COOK

Many people exercise so they can trim the fat or train for a specific goal like a marathon. Truth time: They are entirely missing the point. Personally, we exercise to assuage our cognitive dissonance that appears when we compare all the things we want to eat with all the abs we want to have. This, friends, is precisely why we should all love hiking. In the backcountry, you are constantly in a calorie deficit, which means absolutely nothing is off-limits (as long as you are willing to carry it, of course). S'mores for breakfast? Absolutely. Triple helping of pasta for dinner? Nom nom.

Your cuisine choices are largely a function of the amount of food you are willing to bring and the tools you have available to cook the meal. As such, it is easiest to think about what to make in terms of the four types of dining situations we may encounter.

TYPE 1: DISPERSED CAMPING

Car camping is where you go big. We view every meal as a three-course opportunity to impress our friends, and since we are always camped within arm's reach of the truck, we have every tool we could desire to melt their palates off.

For the starter, stick with something that requires little to no cooking but still plates beautifully. Like a magic show, we use the opening course as a way to distract everyone while we get to work on the entrées. Our go-to appetizer is an oversize charcuterie board with seasonally appropriate fixings, unholy amounts of cheese, and cured meats. Since you are already dining al fresco to the max, get ambitious with the latter: wild boar, lemon-seasoned mussels, elk jerky, and mystery meats have all been well received. Pair this with a highbrow craft beer and you've bought yourself all the time you need to cook your main course.

For the entrée, there are practically no limits. Today's portable propane stoves and grills mean that if you can make it at home, you can likely make it out there, although we prefer to work with old-fashioned campfires and cast iron. Cast-iron goods are the WMDs of the culinary world: Not only are they indestructible (we literally put ours in the fire to cook with it), but slapping an unwelcome campsite guest upside the head with a twelve-inch iron skillet will surely put an end to their existence. We are also huge fans of the Dutch oven (not *that* kind of Dutch oven, calm down) thanks to its downright ease of use. Simply drop in chicken, biscuits, and vegetables, leave it on the campfire while sipping peat-barreled gin for sixty minutes, and voilà! A hefty Southern-inspired dish that will blow minds and arteries with its buttery richness.

Most important, wrap up with a life-changing dessert. There are timeless campfire classics like the aforementioned s'mores, but if you have the gumption and time, produce something more unexpected. Our personal favorite: the cast-iron cookie, for which we fill an entire eight-inch skillet with chocolate chip cookie dough (add chunks of Himalayan sea salt and

caramel if you're feeling spunky) and bake it over the fire. Perfect for sharing, and perfect for the 'Gram.

TYPE 2: BACKPACKING

There is no rule that says you need to live like John Muir and subsist on a steady diet of bread crumbs and expired cheese on the trail. On Heather's first backpacking trip, she carried two cans of soup, three cans of something awful, and one can of beans, which cumulatively weighed more than a small dog. She learned two things: You can carry whatever you want to eat if you want to deal with the weight, and John Muir was likely a stronger hiker than she.

Today our philosophy is simple: Find the foods with the greatest flavor-to-weight ratio. It *is* true that hunger makes the best seasoning, so if we are planning on twenty-mile daily epics, we keep the cuisine simple and prep to a minimum. Hardy steel-cut oatmeal is great for the morning (add fixin's like walnuts and dried cranberries for texture and flavor), lunch consists of bars that can be eaten in transit, and dinners are always dehydrated meals in a bag. We prefer these because they require only boiling water, and cleanup is entirely self-contained, although each bag's 50 percent of your daily value of sodium can eventually take its toll on longer trips. Years ago we packrafted sixty miles on the Alatna River in Gates of the Arctic National Park, and we subsisted solely on dehydrated meals for every calorie on our weeklong endeavor. By the end our internal organs resembled shrunken-head versions of their former selves and our stool was hard-packed enough to form actual furniture (TMI?). But we didn't die of hunger, so it was totally worth it.

Cast-Iron Campfire Cookie

YES, WE CHARACTERIZE IT AS A SINGLE COOKIE; IT'S UP TO YOU IF YOU CARE TO SHARE.

STEP 1: MAKE THE COOKIE DOUGH AT HOME.

Melt 9 tablespoons of butter in a 10-inch cast-iron pan, then let it continue bubbling for about 5 minutes until it becomes brown. Add 3 more tablespoons of butter and melt them in the liquid as well. Transfer the melted mixture into a mixing bowl.

Whisk ¾ cup brown sugar, ½ cup granulated sugar, 2 teaspoons vanilla extract, and 1 heavy teaspoon of salt into the melted butter. We recommend using chunks of Himalayan sea salt—the extra bite in the chunkier bits is divine.

Whisk in an egg plus another egg yolk into the same mixture, and whisk aggressively for 30 seconds (you'll find this part of the process more satisfying if you have a bowl with a mixture attachment). Let it marinate for 3 minutes, whisk for 30 more seconds, marinate for 3 minutes once more, and then give it a final 30 seconds of whisking.

Mix 1¾ cups flour and ½ teaspoon baking soda in a bowl, then add the butter mixture and lovingly mix it until the flour has completely absorbed the mixture.

Add 1½ cups caramel or dark chocolate chips. Or get aggressive and do a mixture of both.

Store the cookie dough in a covered container in the fridge. It should keep for several days, but we advise making it the day before or day of your trip. Be sure to store it in a cooler with ice (preferably in an elevated separate compartment rather than directly on the ice) when in transit to camp.

STEP 2: BAKE THAT COOKIE!

Prep your fire. We typically use the log cabin technique described in chapter 5, as it produces the flame and embers we like for this style of cooking. Ideally you start the fire before dinner so it's burning well by the time you get around to your coup de grâce.

Remove the batter from the cooler and spread it evenly in an 8- or 10-inch cast-iron pan. Cover the pan with foil and place it on a grate over the fire (or drop it right into smoldering embers if you have no grate available). Cook for about 20 minutes, then remove the foil and test the dough with a toothpick. You're welcome to continue cooking if you're unsure it's fully baked, or if you're like Heather and eat raw cookie dough all the time, you can time it to 20 minutes and call it good. Please know that we would never officially advocate eating raw cookie dough.

STEP 3: SERVE THE COOKIE, BLOW SOME MINDS.

After letting it cool for 5 to 15 minutes, cut that beauty into wedges and serve it to your friends. Or if you're splitting it, hand your SO the utensil of their choice and go to town. Don't forget that leftovers could be dangerous for wildlife, so be sure to house the whole thing.

Embarking on more casual trips (think sub-ten miles per day) opens the aperture. Take advantage of perishable goods for the first day or two and bring something extra special for that first meal. Seriously, fresh fruit or vegetables can reconstitute your perspective on the universe! And, once again, so can pizza. Remember that friend who packed in a whole pizza? Let's not forget about him.

You can add a little more flair in camp. There are entire tomes dedicated to the mastery of backpacking meals, but as a starter, remember this: If you can make it at home by simply boiling water, you can make it at camp. Mac 'n' cheese, here we come! As further evidence, one of our favorite camping nightcaps is a homebound classic: Double-boil water in

a nesting titanium bowl set to melt eight ounces of extra-dark chocolate for fondue. Pair with fresh strawberries and a liter of boxed wine that you chilled in a nearby body of water. You can later tell your progeny they are named after the creek their parents camped next to when they conceived in the backcountry. Never miss a chance to embarrass your kids.

We asked the Boulder chef and all-around handsome guy Kyle Mendenhall to create a vegetarian recipe for the backcountry (see next page). He recommends testing the prep as described at home first, then advance to the backcountry option once you get the home prep dialed. Trust us, you'll have volunteers to taste test.

Carrot Chorizo

YIELDS 4 SERVINGS

This recipe is a great vegan option that packs a punch full of flavor. It can stand alone or is a great component to add to almost any meal. I like the chorizo cooked with eggs in the morning or over coal-roasted cabbage with a little feta and toasted pine nuts crumbled on top.

INGREDIENTS

4 cups carrots, peeled

½ tsp whole cumin seed

3 whole cloves

¾ tsp coriander seed

1 tsp smoked black pepper

1 Tbs chili powder

1 tsp garlic powder

a dash dried marjoram

2 ½ tsp salt

¾ tsp Alepo chili

pinch of red pepper flakes

1 Tbs apple cider vinegar

2 ½ tsp olive oil

sunflower oil

OPTIONAL TOPPINGS:

feta cheese

toasted pine nuts

roasted cabbage (cut into wedges)

PREPARATION

At Home

Grind the peeled carrots in a meat grinder or food processor, making sure to save all the juice that the process produces. Set aside while making the spice mix.

Toast the cumin, cloves, coriander, and smoked black pepper in dry sauté pan. Transfer to a mortar or spice grinder and grind. Add the remaining spices and salt, and grind again. Mix the spices and carrots in a large bowl. Add the cider vinegar, then olive oil.

Mix well. Let sit for a few minutes at room temperature. Sauté the carrot mix in a hot pan with a little sunflower oil until the carrots have a little color (caramelization). Serve warm, or cool and store.

For the Backcountry

If you are bringing a stove and pan on your trip, you can bag the mix raw and uncooked. If not, cook it up at home and bag it to take along. Raw or cooked, the carrot mix will last a day unrefrigerated. For a longer trip, freeze the whole bag.

TYPE 3: ULTRALIGHT HIKING

There is a subset of über-hikers who derive immense pleasure from the lightness of their packs as they carefreely ambulate about the woods. They fastidiously track each gram, priding themselves on their half-size toothbrushes and homemade aluminum-can stoves. We have just one piece of advice for this crowd: When we are on day three of our trans-Yosemite hike, don't you dare ask us for an extra pouch of hot chocolate because you were unimpressed with your mug of tepid dandelion tea.

"RECIPE"

Rice cakes and astronaut ice cream. Treat yo'self.

TYPE 4: THE RETURN TO CIVILIZATION

This is your stomach's Shangri-la. After days of borderline sodium over-dosing, you return to the trailhead and have unfettered access to all of the modern world's culinary wonders in the shape of pizza, burgers, and beer. In a likely obvious homage to Hobbits, our crew has a time-honored tradition of "thirdsies" after all of our backcountry ski trips. This involves eating

three full meals at three different restaurants within walking distance of each other. Our favorite trio: sushi, buffalo wings, and an extra-large frozen yogurt. We are confident the Shire-dwellers would be proud.

Don't make the mistake of talking about (or even thinking about) this moment until you are on the home stretch of the last day of your hike. Violating this rule is punishable by social ostracization or getting tarred and feathered, whichever is more convenient.

CHAPTER FIVE

HOW AND WHERE TO BUILD A CAMPFIRE

With all due respect to Chuck Noland, campfires aren't about survival; they are about romance. The crackling aural nostalgia combined with our olfactory system's strong association with memory means we are awash in a lifetime of amazing memories every time we are tucked under a starry sky with friends and a fire. Even more important, we know we will soon be inhaling s'mores, a dessert more iconic than the flames themselves.

TYPES OF WOOD

No matter which layout you choose, each fire will have the following components. Don't try to jump straight to lighting your largest logs. Instead, start small before building up to a roaring flame you can see from several zip codes away.

TINDER

This is the part of your fire that catches easily and burns *fast*. However much tinder you think you need, double it. Getting fires started almost always takes a few more tries than anticipated, and it's bothersome to run out of tinder when you're *this close* to getting your fire off and running. If you are collecting tinder from near camp, look for bark, dry leaves, or splintered wood shavings from a fallen tree. Or perhaps you came prepared, so just light your petroleum jelly–soaked cotton ball (see page 60) and call it a day.

KINDLING

This is the bridge from your quick-burning tinder to your long-burning logs. Look for sticks no girthier than your pinky, and gather a large collection. Reminder: Make sure it's completely dead and dry—if it doesn't snap easily in your hands, it's likely too green and will result in a very unsatisfying smoky mess.

LOGS

This is your primary source of fuel once you get the kindling lit. Bigger is not necessarily better, no matter what the masculine-looking fellow in your party says. Three to four inches in diameter will catch a lot faster than the massive logs seen on your favorite Hallmark movie. Split larger logs with an ax instead; Abe was right when he said chopping your own wood warms you twice—plus, splitting logs in front of your tentmates is deeply satisfying.

HOW TO BUILD A CAMPFIRE

There are several options to build a campfire, each with its own merits. Here are a few commonly used examples that are easy to manage.

THE LOG CABIN

This is our go-to for building all-night fires with groups. For one, it is easy to build, especially when you have a collection of your dearest friends watching and auditing your every move from a safe distance where they aren't doing any real work. Simply line up two logs parallel to each other and then put two more orthogonally on top to create an octothorpe (also known as a "hashtag" by the kids). Repeat this a few more times to build the cabin, set the tinder and kindling in the middle, and ignite. The large logs burn well on their own, and it is easy to continue adding height after the fire has started, even if it's well past midnight and you are halfway through a handle of Woodford Reserve.

THE STAR

If you find yourself in Westworld, consider a star fire. It has been favored by both Native Americans and pioneers for its positive ratio of fuel-to-burn time, which is particularly helpful in western environments where wood isn't as plentiful as back East. This style is specifically designed for a slow burn and uses much less fuel than the log cabin. Although you end up with a more diminutive flame, we've found it sufficient for smaller groups when you want a fire to run all night with minimal maintenance.

Cottonballs as Firestarters If you want an easy DIY fire starter, put a collection of 100-percent-cotton balls and pure petroleum jelly into a sealed plastic bag. Work the jelly into the cotton balls (don't completely saturate them, just get close) before removing and storing them in a hipster film canister. If you don't know what a film canister is, ask your oldest coworker (sorry in advance if you also get a lecture on three-and-a-half-inch disks). Once in camp, you can use the cotton ball as your tinder—it should emit a constant flame for a couple of minutes when lit.

Start by creating a small fire like the teepee (see below), and then arrange five large logs with each of their ends in the fire, all equidistant from each other (hence the star moniker). Once the big logs catch, slowly push them into the center flame to keep them burning over time.

THE TEEPEE

If you were a Girl Scout or Boy Scout, you probably learned this simple approach for creating a small fire. We find it a bit easier to catch aflame than the log cabin, but it does require more maintenance if you plan on the fire burning for several hours. To start, collect a handful of small and medium-size logs and arrange them in a teepee-shaped cone around your kindling. Continue adding logs until you have a continuous wall with one slot to access the kindling. Be warned that as the bigger logs start burning, they will eventually collapse on themselves or potentially fall away from the fire. It isn't an enormous hazard, but it may be moderately sketchy if you have sober children and/or inebriated adults in camp.

THE LEAN-TO

Windchill makes you cold and cold makes you want a fire, but the fire can't handle the wind. It's a cruel world, isn't it? Use this style to start a fire in gusty conditions. Begin with a large log and orient it perpendicular to the primary wind direction. Next assemble your tinder on the leeward side of the log, and arrange a collection of small to medium sticks above the tinder and leaning against the large log. The windbreak will help the small fire get started, and eventually it will burn hot enough to light the large log. Continue adding fuel as needed.

WHERE TO BUILD A CAMPFIRE

Campfires fall into two categories: those built in existing fire rings and those that aren't. Unless it is a matter of life and death, please build fires only in designated sites or previously impacted locations. Fires are beautiful, but they also scar the earth, and a collection of ashen rings mars someone else's backcountry experience. Personally, we build

BUILDING A CAMPFIRE

 ## LOG CABIN

1.

2. (Repeat 1-2x)

↗ KINDLING

3.

 ## THE STAR

1.

↗ KINDLING & MEDIUM LOGS

2.

3.

TEEPEE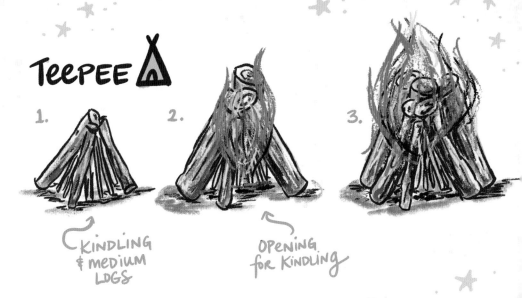

1.

2.

3.

KINDLING
& MEDIUM
LOGS

OPENING
for KINDLING

LEAN-TO

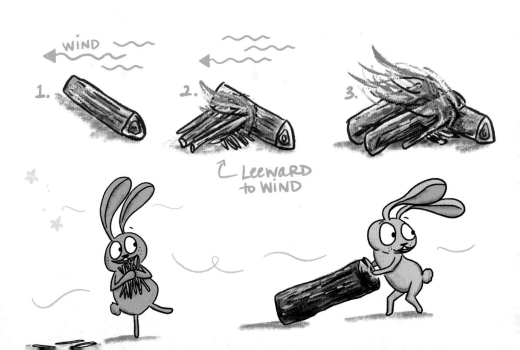

WIND

1.

2.

3.

LEEWARD
to WIND

fires only in existing frontcountry campgrounds or dispersed camping locations with established fire rings. This prevents us from collecting too much firewood in the backcountry (buy the wood locally), and it is much easier to keep gallons of water on hand in case something goes sideways.

CAMPFIRE ETIQUETTE

Campfires are fun and a core part of many folks' outdoors experience. That said, there are a few things to keep in mind every time you start day-dreaming about s'mores.

Burn only local wood. It is easy to pick some up from a gas station near the trailhead or collect downed wood if that is allowed in your area. Bringing wood from other locales may unintentionally introduce a pestilence as a result of stowaway insects, and you don't want that on your conscience.

Don't be an uncouth heathen and build campfires where they shouldn't exist, even if someone else already built a fire ring for your convenience.

Check local rules on when you can burn. Fires frequently are not allowed in the backcountry at high elevations because the local environs rely on nutrients from the dead wood. Additionally, birds and other critters will frequently build homes in downed trees, and they will be very sad if you set their house on fire.

When you're done with a fire, keep pouring water on it until it's completely out: The ashes should be cool to the touch. This will take much longer than you think, so start the process about twenty minutes before you plan on getting horizontal. If you don't have water available, disperse the embers with a poker and stir them in the dirt until they completely extinguish. Making the front-page news is great unless an editor

is putting you above the fold because you're mentally deficient and an ember from your fire burned thousands of acres.

And for the love of everything holy, if you are anywhere near wildfire season, think *very* hard about whether or not a campfire is a good idea. Spoiler: It probably isn't.

CHAPTER SIX

HOW TO PICK A BACKCOUNTRY CAMPSITE

America is blessed with some of the most diverse and remarkable natural wonders in the world. Prior to our founding, nations established that the most spectacular properties were reserved for the elite (that is, a royal family's private hunting grounds), and the concept of wide swaths of nationally managed public land was essentially unheard of prior to the opening of Yellowstone National Park in the late 1800s. Yet thanks to the foresight of a collection of noble folks, they set the precedent that continues to protect millions upon millions of acres for everyone to enjoy, both domestically and abroad.

It's important to remember that our public lands were not here first. Many of our most treasured spaces were and still are sacred to Indigenous Peoples; Yosemite Valley was a place of significance well before Camp 4 produced climbing deities like Royal Robbins and Peter Croft. So as you plan out your trip, take a beat to do some research to learn about the history of a place and its people. Connect with someone locally if you can, and please treat them and their ancestral home with the respect they deserve.

We can tell you exactly where to find our favorite campsite in the world: the north side of Thousand Island Lake in the Ansel Adams Wilderness. This protected area (née the Minarets Wilderness in 1964 as part of the Wilderness Act) abuts the southern end of Yosemite and essentially main-

tains all of the park's high-country beauty without any of its roads. The campsite itself was Will's first overnight destination in the Sierras, and it entirely changed his perspective on what it means to be in wilderness. The site sits elevated above the 9,833-foot-high Thousand Island and it has clear views of the Ritter Range. With its eastern-facing peaks unobstructed by anything between the horizon and their summits, sunrise here is as good as it gets. The alpenglow reflected in the lake, the lupine and Indian paintbrush along the shoreline, and benign Sierra summer temps are pure magic. When we are looking for a campsite, this is the standard to which we hold all others.

The views aren't everything, however. Natural shade, lack of mosquitoes, morning sun on the tent, flat ground—the list goes on. There are many other factors to consider, and you may personally be willing to trade.

CAMPSITE CONSIDERATIONS IN THE BACKCOUNTRY

No matter what, please choose a campsite that is designated for camping or has a durable surface like a slab of granite or dry dirt. We get it; there is serious temptation to set up camp in a beautiful alpine meadow that puts you in the middle of a Thomas Kinkade painting. We promise there are numerous other opportunities to get the IG shot that demonstrates how outdoorsy you are.

We always prioritize views over water, but if you don't like the idea of schlepping from a river or lake back to camp every time you need fresh H_2O, you may want to consider posting up somewhere closer. Be sure to check local regulations on how far to camp from a body of water (and keep in mind that insects like moisture too).

At the risk of being obvious, choose somewhere flat. Even if it is a slight incline, you will end up logrolling with your tentmates all night owing to the slipperiness of your nylon sleeping bag. If you can't find some-

where perfectly flat, at least endeavor to put your head on the uphill side (which also prevents your blood from pooling in your noggin).

Take a good look at your proposed site and imagine what would happen if it starts raining. You certainly don't want to camp in something like a wash (although the sandy bottoms are delightfully soft) or do what one of our friends did a few years back in Canyonlands National Park. We were exhausted after day one of our packrafting trip, and after spending all day out on the Green River in full sun, we hardly had the gumption to do an extensive search for a campsite. We camped in the first open area we found, but our friends had the strong desire to find some shade trees as natural blackout curtains. As a result, the duo camped in a small, low-lying grove. Several hours later, an early summer storm blew through the area. Thankfully, there was no thunder so we slept through it. Imagine our surprise when we awoke in the morning to a bluebird sky and our friends' tent a couple hundred meters from where it was the previous night. Turns out, they were forced to move the shelter during the heat of the storm when they found their sundries floating inside of the tent in nearly two inches of water. Life lesson: Don't pitch your tent in a bowl.

If you are summertime camping in the mountains, sleep high. The number one reason: vicious skeeters. These life-sucking monstrosities can turn even the loveliest of trips sideways, but higher elevations typically have a consistent breeze to keep the bugs at bay. Plus, cold air collects in natural low points like the meadow referenced above. Even if everything feels perfectly cozy when you are first crawling into bed, you are going to be pretty sad come three a.m.

If you plan on an early start, find a spot that faces east. The rising sun will warm you up faster and you won't have to bother setting an alarm clock.

Avoid camping under dead trees, or hiking under them in general. There is a reason they're called widow makers.

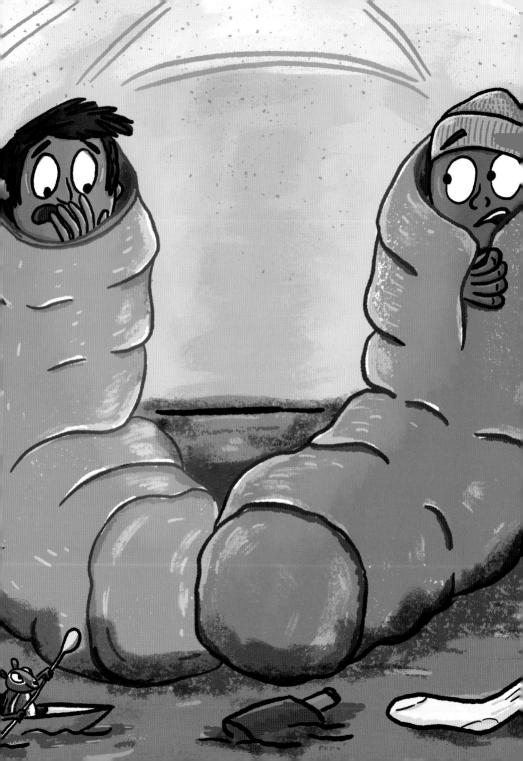

OUR FAVORITE BACKCOUNTRY CAMPSITES

To be fair, the majority of our domestic backcountry experiences are in the American West, and we're confident this list could start an aggressive bar argument in Boulder or Portland. But if we include nostalgia as a critical portion of the rubric, here is a semi-complete list of our current favorite spots to backcountry camp in the United States and Canada (not including the aforementioned site, of course).

BRINS MESA, RED ROCK SECRET MOUNTAIN WILDERNESS, SEDONA, ARIZONA

We met in Sedona at a press event for outdoor journalists, but it took us six years to return and hike together here. One small adjustment: This time we had an extra fifteen-pound weight in our packs known as our six-month-old daughter. Admittedly, sentimentality is likely why we love this campsite so much, but truly, it is that good. It was our first overnight trip with progeny, and even though we were a short 2.3 miles from the trailhead, it felt like an enormous achievement that all three of us survived. Superlatives are insufficient when it comes to describing the mesa's views as you enjoy unadulterated panoramas of Sedona's famous red rock in every direction. It is astounding any time of day, but sunset and sunrise are especially stunning. One important note: Be sure to hike far enough along the mesa to ensure you are out of the restricted camping area. This hike is perfect for those who are looking to test their overnight mettle, since it is a short jaunt and close to town, but the trade-off is that it isn't as deep into the backcountry as others.

THE ALATNA RIVER, GATES OF THE ARCTIC NATIONAL PARK, ALASKA

On the other hand, this site is about as backcountry as it gets. Alaska's Gates of the Arctic National Park is perched on top of our planet just north of the Arctic Circle, and it is roughly 13,000 square miles without a single

trail (Rhode Island is about 1,200 square miles, to offer some perspective). This packrafting trip epitomized Type 2 fun: At the time, we thought paddling into rainy headwinds in near-freezing temps was about the most awful thing you could do (and to think, we spent our hard-earned money to get the opportunity to do this). But with the passage of time and inclement weather, we look back on those mornings camped along the bank of the Alatna as some of our favorite memories. The riverside was coated in grizzly prints, and one small bear even ran through camp! Knowing our only way home was via a bush plane sixty miles downstream really spiked the "Oh #@$%, we are *out* here" feeling, but that's what makes it special.

SECOND LAKE, EASTERN SIERRA, CALIFORNIA

This is objectively the best bang-for-buck backcountry hike of all time. For less than five miles one way you are rewarded with a picture-perfect granite bench overlooking the exceedingly picturesque Temple Crag as it lords over a glacier-fed emerald lake. Perfection.

LULU KEY, 10,000 ISLANDS NATIONAL WILDLIFE REFUGE, FLORIDA

There are dozens of keys along Florida's southern coast, but we love this one because its south-facing orientation gives you a front-row seat to sunrise *and* sunset from the same camping spot during the winter months. And trust us, you want to go during the winter when temps are benign. If you travel during the summer, the pterodactyl-size mosquitoes will carry you and your gear away. Time it right and you may get lucky; it is quite possible to have the island entirely to yourself.

CHIMNEY POND, BAXTER STATE PARK, MAINE

Chimney Pond is different from others on this list because it's a backcountry campground, meaning you still hike just over three miles to get there. But when you arrive, you will find nine lean-to shelters and a bunkhouse that sleeps ten people. Thanks to the relatively plush accommodations, Chimney Pond is an awesome option for families or new hikers who aren't quite ready to commit to that whole sleeping-on-the-ground thing.

FAVORITE BACKCOUNTRY CAMPSITES

ALATNA RIVER

AK

Hole-in-the-WALL

BUCKSKIN GULCH

ICE LAKES BASIN

MT

CA

UT

CO

AZ

FL

SECOND LAKE

HAVASU FALLS

BRINS MESA

LULU KEY 10,000 ISLANDS

CONFLUENCE OF THE BUCKSKIN GULCH
AND PARIA RIVER, UTAH

Buckskin is a life-changing hike in itself, and its slot canyons, dry falls, and Cesspool (promise, it is a proper noun) are the stuff of which dreams are made. Overlooked, however, is one of our favorite campsites. After hiking about a dozen miles, you arrive at an enormous amphitheater with near-vertical red rock walls. Once the sun goes down, it gets so dark that you can't see your hand in front of your face. Lie down next to your tent and enjoy the triangular cutout of stars above.

ICE LAKES BASIN, COLORADO

Wildflowers, unearthly blue lakes, spiny ridgelines—this is classic southern Colorado. Set in a picturesque alpine bowl at roughly 12,000 feet, this isn't a hike for the timid, but the stunning surroundings more than make up for the sweat equity. Pitch your tent near any of the aqua-colored lakes and marvel at the craggy yet colorful 13,000-foot peaks surrounding the bowl. It's almost like Narnia, only better.

HAVASU FALLS, ARIZONA

We may have met in Sedona, but our first overnight hiking trip was near Havasu Falls on the Havasupai Indian Reservation. You won't have this Insta-famous place to yourself, but it doesn't matter—the travertine waters are worth sharing. Set up shop and don't bother moving your tent for a few days, as there are plenty of day trips to enjoy exploring the canyon, rivers, and falls. Pro tip: Avoid this hike in the dead heat of summer. Scorching doesn't even begin to describe those temps.

HOLE-IN-THE-WALL,
GLACIER NATIONAL PARK, MONTANA

This one is not easy to get to, both in terms of distance and nabbing permits. But sweet goodness, the juice is worth the squeeze. The camp is improbably perched in a basin that sits above a cliff band, making every site feel like it is on the edge of the world. If you've visited the Rockies in

Colorado, the range up north has an entirely different feel. Although they are lower in elevation, the peaks themselves are hulking, and this provides one of the best seats in the house to see them up close.

GREAT SAND DUNES NATIONAL PARK, COLORADO

Okay, camping in the sand isn't for everyone, so we're fairly positive you may revolt when we suggest hiking through the grainy stuff. But hear us out: Backcountry camping in Great Sand Dunes is an otherwordly experience that more than makes up for the arduous hiking conditions. Permits are limited; last we heard, only twenty per day are available, so get to the Ranger Station ASAP. Once you're there, the rangers will give you some life advice on how not to die out there (for example, begin hiking at five p.m., when the sand temps have fallen to lower than that of a frying pan). Thankfully, the rule is that you only need to hike until you cannot see the visitor center anymore. There aren't any trails (because it's sand, duh) so you're guaranteed an utterly peaceful evening with the best star show on the planet.

ALICE-TOXAWAY LOOP, THE SAWTOOTHS, IDAHO

This three-day, nineteen-mile loop is quintessential Sawtooth and has become a thing of lore in the backpacking world. To be clear, this is not a route for beginners: Hikers will experience river crossings, steep climbs, and quad-busting descents. But if you're feeling sprightly and up for the task, the Sawtooths are easily one of the most beautiful places on the planet. Insider tip: Prepare to strip down to your skivvies at least once or twice. Diving into the pristine glacial water is a must-have experience on your life list.

VALHALLA PROVINCIAL PARK, BRITISH COLUMBIA, CANADA

The Valhallas are the type of peaks that make your jaw drop the first time you see them. They're *that* beautiful. When combined with Canadian hospitality, next to no tourist traffic, and scores of friendly mountain goats with an insatiable curiosity, Valhalla Provincial Park is tough to beat for

anyone looking for a couple of nights away from civilization. Most of the routes in the park aren't mellow, or easily accessible. Be prepared to drive. But once you've been exposed to the alpine wonderland packed full of granite spires and majestic lakes tucked into unassuming valleys, you'll quickly forget how long it took you to get there. You're just psyched that you made it.

CHAPTER SEVEN

TYPES OF SHELTER

We already talked about the various styles of camping in chapter 2, but let's pretend for a minute that you're ready to take the plunge: You want to camp outside in a tent. That opens up an entirely new can of worms, because walking the tent aisle at a local outdoor shop can be as confusing as reading the nutrition label on a bag of

cookies. What do these words mean? Why are there so many syllables? WHY IS SLEEPING OUTSIDE SO COMPLICATED?

Slow your roll. Once you understand a few of the basics, shelter lingo won't confuse you. Instead, you may even find yourself talking shop with store employees, debating the pros and cons of single-wall versus double-wall tents.

Or maybe not.

BIVY SACKS

Envision this: Dig around under your sink for a trash bag, spread it out, climb inside of it with your sleeping bag, and find an errant stick to prop up the bag above your face. Oh, and maybe cut a small hole somewhere so you can breathe. Sound good?

This is the world of bivy sacks, the let's-hope-you-don't-ever-actually-need-this item. Rarely called by its full name (bivouac sack), this is designed to be no more than a waterproof breathable cover for your sleeping bag. As the bare minimum in backcountry shelters, no one really wants to sleep in a bivy sack since they are small, claustrophobic, and lonely.

But in a pinch, bivy sacks make great emergency shelters to ride out an unplanned night outdoors.

TARP SHELTERS

The next lightest camping option behind bivy sacks is a tarp shelter. Designed just like a shade tarp, these are typically floorless and require a pole or various guylines to stake out a type of awning above your head. Tarp shelters keep rain and snow off you, but they don't provide much protection in the way of creepy-crawlies. If you have a strong aversion to sleeping in the dirt with insects, you may do better with a tent.

But, as with any type of shelter, the trade-offs may be worth it. While tarp shelters lack conventional protection, they are much lighter than tents. You can easily roll up a shelter, shove it in the bottom of your backpack, and trek on your merry way without fretting about the weight. Worth it? Some think so, and many thru-hikers swear by tarp shelters.

HAMMOCKS

How do you know if you've met a hammock camper? They will tell you, loudly and proudly.

BIVY

TYPES
OF SHELTER

TARP

HAMMOCK

SINGLE-WALL TENT

DOUBLE-WALL TENT

But seriously, hammock enthusiasts are a growing breed who staunchly advocate for sleeping in the air versus sleeping on terra firma. And they're not wrong: There is something distinctly comfortable about floating when compared to the unforgiving ground. Plus, some argue that pitching a hammock is eleventy billion times easier than pitching a tent; you don't need to worry about rocks, roots, or even a flat surface (although you'll be hosed if you try to pitch a hammock above tree line or in the desert).

All that said, hammock camping comes with separate complications. Since you don't have a vestibule as you would with a tent, you won't likely have anywhere protected to store your gear. Basic hammocks don't offer any weather protection either, although newer, streamlined models come with bug netting and/or waterproof tarps so that you can truly get outside in all weather. And here's another factor: Since cool air blows underneath the hammock all night, they do sleep cold. Depending on the weather and your overnight low temperatures, you may need to look into sleeping pads or underquilts specifically designed for hammockers.

TENTS

And now we get to the king of the shelters: the almighty tent. In general, tents can be broken into two categories: single wall and double.

SINGLE-WALL TENTS

Single-wall shelters are similar to tarp shelters except that they weigh more because they have standard tent features like a floor and door. But the entire body for the tent is constructed from one layer of material, which means that they are usually lighter than double-wall tents (see below). This is possible thanks to various technologies that combine waterproofing and breathability into one layer.

The benefits of single-wall shelters are obvious: They're lightweight, offer full weather protection, and are easy to set up in nasty weather since you don't have to worry about a rainfly. But the single-layer construction isn't as breathable as mesh, so condensation frequently builds up, making the inside of the tent toastier than a sweat lodge. This type of shelter is quite popular with mountaineers and hardcore backpackers, but it usually costs a chunk of money, so entry-level campers may want to consider a double wall.

DOUBLE-WALL TENTS

Double-wall tents are likely what you've seen in any movie, or may be the only type of shelter you have personally experienced. The not-so-secret is in the name: This type of shelter construction uses two layers of material rather than one. Typically, double walls have an inner tent and a rainfly. The inner tent usually has some mesh on the walls for breathability along with a waterproof floor. Then a second waterproof layer called the rainfly goes over the top to keep Mother Nature out. Easy peasy.

Since there is more material on a double-wall tent, these are usually heavier than single-wall shelters. But they provide a bit more flexibility. Want to canoodle during a romantic evening under the stars? Ditch the rainfly and stargaze through the mesh. Desert camping and the sun is beating down on you? Deploy the rainfly halfway so that you have a shady side of the tent to enjoy. More often than not, larger car camping tents are double-wall shelters, which makes them great options for family frolicking weekends. We certainly don't like to make assumptions, but our guess is that if you snagged a copy of this book, you likely are looking at double walls.

CHAPTER EIGHT

WHAT TO WEAR

Most weather is hiking weather if you have the right apparel. If you are looking for an excuse to triple your gear closet, this chapter will help you justify increasing your quiver when your significant other starts questioning your purchases.

This chapter focuses on the apparel you should wear to stay comfortable. Each subsection isn't intended to be an all-inclusive list. For example, we don't talk about sunglasses or variations of grape smugglers; rather, we get into the elements of each wardrobe that are particular to those types of conditions.

HOT DAYS

As contradictory as this sounds, one of the best things you can do to stay comfortable under the blazing hot sun is put on more clothes. Once you get to your alpine lake or waterfall, there's plenty of time to strip to your underwear and get your high-altitude tan on. In the meantime, our go-to sun kit includes a loose-fitting, long-sleeved sun hoodie (these are very lightweight shirts, not sweatshirt hoodies), trucker hat, and pants.

Obviously this attire will prevent sunburns—wearing a pack with a sunburn is *the worst*—but without getting too deep into the science, loose apparel allows for airflow that pulls sweat off your skin and thus helps keep you cool. It is the sweat's evaporation that lowers your temp, so put your skin in the shade of its own garment and let that sweet saltiness dissipate. On a personal note, we also strongly prefer sun protection via clothing instead of via sunscreen when we're on longer trips. The sensation of crawling into a sleeping bag and feeling your sunscreen-laden legs and arms stick to the liner is the emotional equivalent of going feet first into the sarlacc. *Hard pass.*

Also, if you are going to stay active from dawn to dusk, plan on consuming about a gallon of water per person per day. Being well dressed counts for naught if you are dehydrated and hallucinating.

COLD DAYS

You've likely heard "They say you should dress in layers" when it comes to hiking in colder climes, right? The mysterious "they" (who seem to espouse universal advice on all kinds of subjects) are right. Think of your cold-weather apparel system in three components: a base layer, an insulating layer, and a shell layer. You might not wear all three all of the time, and depending on the temps and how hard you're working, you might not want to. There is a charming adage from arctic exploration that says, "You sweat, you die." Although you are not likely going Ernest Shackleton on your first trip, it is still sound advice. One of Will's more memorable

trips to the Palisades in the Eastern Sierra involved this lesson. Through a series of unfortunate events, his group started from the parking lot well after dark. After about half a mile of steady uphill, the new guy in the group asked, "Hey, is anyone else hot?" Everyone else said no, which is when he casually mentioned that he was wearing everything he brought, but since he was so warm, he didn't want to stop. Four miles later at camp, he hung all of his apparel from a shoestring in his tent in an effort to do a little line drying. Lamentably, he awoke to discover that everything had frozen solid because it was completely soaked with sweat. Although he did not perish from the earth, he was essentially dead to the group, since no one saw him during the three days of base camping in the valley.

To explain a basic layering system: A base layer is what you wear next to skin. Wool blends have gained significantly in popularity over the past decade, although there are plenty of synthetics that perform admirably. Regardless of material, we prefer it close-fitting in case you need to comfortably wear it underneath other layers. The insulating layer (or midlayer) is typically a lightweight top with down or synthetic insulation; the volume of insulation will depend on how much warmth you want. This is frequently the piece that comes in and out of the pack multiple times a day as conditions shift—your comfort and need for warmth on an exposed, windy ridgeline may be completely different than in the wooded, protected forest at the start of a hike. Finally, your shell layer protects you from precip and wind. Some insulating layers are little more than ultralight nylon shells with a pound of down and some zippers, so they'll do nothing to protect you from windchill. Others have integrated windproof fabric. The important takeaway here is that you build a system of pieces that work well together. There are some apparel pieces that combine insulation and shells, and there are midlayers that have buttery next-to-skin feel. The three elements of base layer, insulation, and shell may not always be three distinct items, but you want to make sure to account for them and their respective technical features when planning your kit.

Of course, there are myriad accessories for managing warmth. At a bare minimum, proper gloves and a beanie can make the difference between a delightful and a miserable trip. A neck gaiter, balaclava, or even an old-fashioned scarf all do an incredible job of keeping well-earned heat from escaping out the top of your jacket. We've even tested remote-controlled heated insoles in subzero temps (they're quite nice, although not entirely necessary). If nothing else, keep a couple of spare hand-warmer packets nearby; functioning digits can mean the difference between successfully operating zippers and just peeing your pants because you don't want to deal with it.

A few final pieces of advice on cold weather:

Stay hydrated. Even if you've successfully managed your sweat, you are still losing fluids.

If you are staying overnight, bring a set of dry base layers (including socks) to change into at camp, and do it the moment you arrive. Base layers do a remarkable job of pulling water vapor away from your epidermis, but they also retain that moisture in the garment, which becomes notably chilly when you stop working as hard in camp. Yes, changing into fresh clothes when it's twenty degrees outside is undesirable, but standing around in wet clothes is even worse.

If you are comfortably warm in the parking lot, you're probably going to overheat within half a mile of starting your hike. Consider starting slightly chilled if you don't want to stop your entire group to change when you're only fifteen minutes into your hike. Or, if you are like Heather and hate being cold and know this about yourself, plan for a pit stop to shed those layers. Regardless, the takeaway is the same: Don't end up like our friend and his frozen clothes.

If you are hiking on snow, take eye protection and sun protection very, very seriously. The UV reflection off the snow's surface is almost as strong as getting it directly from the sun, and snow blindness (that is, when your eyes get sunburned) can set in quickly.

RAINY DAYS

Hiking through extended rain is an endurance test of intestinal fortitude. One of the formative moments of our relationship involved three days straight of driving Alaska rain in temps just barely above freezing (the worst hiking conditions ever, in our opinion). Although we can't really remember what any of the terrain looked like, we did arrive in camp completely dry every night. If you can crawl into a tent and remain nice and dry, everything will be okay. Additionally, the sound of rain on the tent fly while you stretch out comfortably in your fortress of nylon is one of the most romantic sounds on earth, although Heather is still debating its aphrodisiac powers.

When it comes to staying dry, there are a few commonsense pieces of advice worth offering:

Once you're wet, it's a lot harder to get dry again. If you think a storm is rolling in, take the time to get all of your waterproof gear on *before* it starts raining. This also keeps you from fishing around in an open pack while it's precipitating.

Not all waterproof hiking gear is created equal. You could hike in a plastic garbage bag that would likely keep you dry, but you'd find the breathability wanting (although it may be a great way to diet). You could write an entire book on the nuances of water-resistant versus waterproof, and different brands have different definitions of what it means to be waterproof. It's confusing, so here is the short version: If you want something to keep you dry in the worst conditions, choose the most waterproof *and* breathable three-layer material you can find. Water-resistant and two-layer gear will wet out (saturate) faster, and once that happens, it loses its ability to keep you dry.

Yes, waterproof pants are awesome. Like husbands, they can seem superfluous until the day you need them and they finally prove their worth. Even if it isn't raining, they can be significantly more comfortable if you're hiking through vegetative areas covered with dew.

Our hardcore hiking friends swear by umbrellas, and they have a pretty good case for them. For starters, you can get them out in a heartbeat during summer squalls, and you won't have to deal with constantly changing in and out of waterproof gear as the weather shifts. Additionally, they keep your pack and gear dry without the need for a separate cover. They also make excellent shade if you somehow find yourself getting fried by the sun. Finally, as an added bonus, you can enthusiastically sing "A Spoonful of Sugar" and feel moderately justified in doing so.

Pack your sleeping bag in a separate waterproof stuff sack. Most brands include just a lightweight stuff sack, so this will be an aftermarket purchase. Down loses its ability to insulate once it gets wet, which is a total bummer. Even if you have a sleeping bag with synthetic fill, a dry bag is much more pleasurable than a damp one.

CHAPTER NINE

NAVIGATION BASICS

Getting lost is not as easy as it used to be. For some, this is a blessing: Our national parks and similar wilderness areas are so well marked that if you have a map and a basic ability to tell up from down, you can do just fine on most hikes. We've crisscrossed all over the world and never owned a GPS unit (aside from a sweet car-mount TomTom), and as long as we've stayed on trails we've needed only a compass and map.

All that said, it would be foolish to not brush up on some basics before you go out, and especially if you ever amble into cross-country hiking. The most lost Will has ever been in his life involved his first cross-country hike in the Sierra, inspired by an article from *Backpacker* magazine in the early aughts. It described a route through Evolution Basin, which is the kind of hidden gem whose natural beauty is beyond compare. To make a long story medium in length, the crew split into two groups of two on the last day so the faster party could get to the car earlier and drive it up to the trailhead, which would spare the second group four miles of hiking on the road. Lamentably, they had only a single map among them. When the first group went without it, they accidentally ascended the wrong col and hiked over talus and scree for nearly a full day in the wrong direction. Seeing the lesson here? Maps are useful.

Since this chapter covers the basics, let's start with the most obvious: Stick to well-marked, well-mapped trails, and this is relatively straightforward. You can practice all of these skills with a safety net, and should you ever endeavor to pursue cross-country hiking, be sure to bring more than one map.

THE MAP AND COMPASS

Maps are intoxicating. There are so many *possibilities* with a quality map. We have an embarrassingly large collection of them; some are of places we've been, some of places we'd like to go, and some simply as lovely décor. For hiking specifically, you want a topo map. This is short for *topographical,* and it is important because it doesn't just show you trails, but also communicates terrain. Back in the day, these were referred to as quads because the United States Geological Survey divided everything into topographical quadrants, so if you were headed somewhere that didn't have a designated map for the area (like a famous national park), you had to assemble a collection of quads to cover all the terrain you planned to hike. Today you can have custom maps printed in almost any orientation, but the basics of reading a topo remain the same.

Start by examining the contour lines. The closer the lines are drawn on a two-dimensional map, the steeper the terrain (many maps have shading to assist with this visualization). Once you can visualize the terrain, you'll see obvious meadows, peaks, and similar terrestrial landmarks that may help you triangulate your position. You can also look at topo maps to identify new trails for cross-country routes where they are allowed; keep

RULER

DIRECTION of TRAVEL ARROW

ORIENTING ARROW

READ HERE

BEARING MARK

DECLINATION ADJUSTMENT

ORIENTING LINES

AZIMUTH RING

in mind that although the terrain appears low grade on the map, it may be covered with vegetation that makes passage nearly impossible. Also, remember that contour lines are like Kim Kardashian and Kris Humphries –they should never intersect. Finally, many maps highlight the miles between trail junctions and other points of interest, but if you need to get a different assessment of distance, use the scale and a string to measure out the miles. Also, different maps may have different scales; we prefer smaller maps with more detail for unfamiliar terrain, as larger maps may make it difficult to read details in the contour lines.

Now that you can read a map, let's talk about how to find yourself on it. First of all, make sure you have a proper compass. This doesn't mean you need one of the über-fancy ones that cost hundreds of dollars (although you'll really impress your bushcraft friends), but it should have some basic components:

Ruler: Don't eyeball the scale on the map. Be precise.

Direction of travel arrow: It seems simple, but you want a means to make it obvious which way you are headed when you are taking a bearing.

Bearing mark: Speaking of, you'll want a small mark at the top of the compass rose that tells you where to read your bearing.

Azimuth ring: This rotating ring around the compass rose adjusts so you can set your bearing relative to the magnetic north.

Orienting lines: These lines are usually inside the ring, and they rotate with it so you can align north/south on the map with the compass.

Orienting arrow: Similarly, there should be an arrow inside the ring that you use to align the needle. Because it rotates with the ring, this is what you use to align the azimuth ring with magnetic north.

Declination adjustment: Do not skip this. In some places the difference between magnetic north and true north is negligible, but the farther north you go in the United States, the more drastic the difference between the two. To explain it briefly, your compass will always point toward the magnetic north pole, which is around three hundred miles away from the actual north pole of the planet. If you're hiking near Seattle, for example, there can be a fifteen-degree difference between the two. To put that in perspective, just a single degree can make the difference of one hundred feet over the course of a mile. The ways to adjust declination vary by compass, but make sure you do it before you leave the trailhead. You can usually find the declination printed on most maps, but keep in mind it can change over time, so make sure you get a recent reading.

Now that you have a proper compass and map, let's get the map oriented. This will feel natural to most folks, but to be prescriptive about it . . .

Step 1: Friendly reminder: Double-check that you've correctly adjusted for declination in your zone.

Step 2: Put your compass on your map and make sure the edge of the compass is aligned with the left or right edge of the map (assuming north is top/front of your map). The direction of travel arrow should also be pointed the same direction as north on your map.

Step 3: Turn the ring so there's a nice alignment between the direction of travel arrow and the "N" on the azimuth ring.

Step 4: Holding the compass against the map, turn your body until the magnetic arrow aligns with the orienting arrow. You should now have alignment among north on your map, north on the azimuth ring, the direction of travel arrow, the orienting arrow, the bearing mark, and the magnetic arrow.

Well done—your map is now pointed the same direction as the landscape in front of you! But guess what: We're not done yet. Now let's learn how to find where *you* are on the map. After all, it's tough to figure out where to go if you don't know where you are, right?

Step 1: In some cases this may be relatively obvious. If you are on a well-known pass, by the confluence of a river or similar obvious landmark,

you can likely find where you are relatively quickly. Use times like this to double-check your triangulation skills where the penalty for failure is pretty low.

Step 2: You'll want to stop somewhere where you can see several obvious natural landmarks. Ideally you want three, and you want them to be at least 60 degrees apart from each other. Start by getting a bearing toward your first landmark by holding the compass level and pointing the direction of travel arrow directly at the landmark. Rotate the ring until the orienting arrow is aligned with the magnetic arrow, and then check the bearing mark to get a reading.

Step 3: Now set the compass back on your map (it is still oriented north, right?), and align the top corner of the compass with the landmark on the map. With the corner of the compass anchored on the landmark, rotate the entire compass until the orienting lines inside the azimuth ring align with north/south on your map. Congratulations—you are located somewhere along the imaginary line that runs along the edge of the compass and connects to the landmark!

Step 4: To find your location, repeat the same process with a second landmark that is at least 60 degrees removed from the first. Do the same with a third, and the three imaginary lines should generate a small triangular swath of land that represents where you are. If it does *not* create a small triangle, you should consider double-checking your math.

A friendly reminder about bearings: Unlike magnetic north, a bearing is a relative direction between your current position and a future destination. Said another way, you can't tell someone who's in a different spot on the trail to follow your same bearing and have them arrive at the same destination.

That wasn't so terrible, was it? But we can already hear you asking: *What about GPS units? Aren't those much easier?* GPS is a wonderful thing, and it has saved our tail more than once when navigating on snow (when we couldn't find the trail) or canoeing through the backcountry. We will borrow a GPS when we're headed out on a trip in which we expect navigation challenges, as it is a wonderful way to double-check our navigation skills as we go. That said, don't let it become too much of a crutch. Aside from the obvious fact that electronics can and will fail in the backcountry, relying on a GPS also may prevent you from constantly forming a mental map while you're hiking. Having a sense of direction is something that's built over the course of your hike, and you must constantly double-check your location, bearing, and landmarks to form this mental reference. Yes, this sentiment can make you seem like a crotchety old curmudgeon who doesn't believe in newfangled tech. Get off my lawn.

PAY ATTENTION

Make a point to consistently take note of where you are and the appearance of the surrounding terrain, including looking behind you. This is especially true for out-and-back hikes that involve summits above tree line, as landmarks become much less obvious once you get into boulders, scree, and snow. Colorado is famous for its fourteeners, and in the summertime, it's consistently a race to the top and back down before the usual thunderstorms roll in. The area may be well trammeled with various social trails (informal, unsanctioned trails created by hikers), and if you're in a hurry to beat an impending hailstorm (which we've done on numerous occasions), you don't want to second-guess your route because it doesn't look familiar.

Also, make time to consistently check your map and double-check your course. It's easy to get in the mind-set of "I'm pretty sure I know where I'm going," which is a good way to end up a few miles in the wrong direction. Keep your map and compass handy for frequent spot checks; if they're buried in your pack, you'll rarely get around to using them when you should.

OKAY, BUT I AM LOST. NOW WHAT?

At some point this will likely happen to you. The first thing: Take a deep breath. Quell any concern or panic that might be festering, as such emotions may force you into a decision that's rash (or at least less thought out than it should be). Stay where you are and assess the situation. Should you remain in your current place and wait for rescue, or are you confident enough to retrace your steps to your last known position? There is absolutely no shame in staying put, especially if it is getting dark and the terrain is steep or otherwise dangerous. In fact, that's certainly the smart bet. Assuming you have the Ten Essentials with you, you likely have enough shelter to spend the night, and it's much easier to hike out on an empty stomach than a broken femur.

Take out your map, get oriented, and see if you can triangulate your current position. Frequently the easiest thing to do is to retrace your steps to the trail, but if going back is not an option, you need to figure out where you are and determine the easiest route to get to your destination. Keep in mind that the easiest route is not necessarily the shortest, but you're much better off choosing the path of least resistance.

Finally, double-check that you aren't operating with location bias. This was how Will became so lost in the earlier story: He assumed he *must*

have ascended the col to the north when he actually ascended the col to the northeast. It was a subtle difference at the start, but after six hours of consistently hiking in the wrong direction (and convincing himself the landmarks he saw were different peaks than they truly were), it took a pair of Europeans he crossed on the trail to convince him otherwise.

As a final reminder, always leave an itinerary and agenda with someone back home. The backcountry is a wild, big place, and search-and-rescue teams will work much more efficiently if they know your intended route.

CHAPTER TEN

MAKING GOOD CHOICES AROUND WILDLIFE

Every campsite was coated in grizzly prints and a small berm separated us from the main flow of the Alatna River. Will woke up a few minutes before everyone else to retrieve our bear canisters from their separate storage location on the other side of the berm. As he was walking back in the predawn light with a canister awkwardly squeezed under each arm, a juvenile grizzly bear appeared on the riverbank about twenty-five yards away. The grizz was ostensibly looking for fish, and given the location in the park, there's a reasonable chance it had never seen a human before. The grizz spotted Will before he had a chance to react, and it thankfully responded in a favorable way for a creature who had never before seen a biped in a bright blue Gore-Tex shell: It turned and sprinted the other direction. This was a relief except for one problem. That direction was right back into camp, and Heather was still in the tent.

Grizzly bears can sprint up to forty miles per hour, but you really can't imagine how fast that is until you see it for yourself. The bear disappeared over the berm, and after a few heart-stopping moments of unintelligible hollering by Will, Heather heard the aural equivalent of E. Honda cannon-balling into a hot tub. The bear had crossed the creek full-tilt, climbed the far bank in two quick moves, and disappeared into the brush. Pucker factor = all-time high.

Seeing wildlife in their natural habitat, especially megafauna, is one of the highlights of being out in the backcountry. Attacks can be serious, but they're also rare, and frequently an attack is the result of errant human be-havior. We'll delve into recommended behaviors around specific species below, but here are a few things that are universally true:

If they react to your presence, you're too close. The general rule in the United States is one hundred yards for bears and wolves, twenty-five

yards for everything else. Consider buying some binoculars and a zoom lens so you may stay a little farther away.

Never feed wildlife, either intentionally or inadvertently. We get it—it's really tempting to feed your extra carrot to a moose, or watch a murder of crows gather round as you spread seeds on the ground. But this creates bad behavior and can ultimately result in the animals' death, because a dependence on human food doesn't provide the nutrition they need. Or, even worse: They get aggressive and they're euthanized, which is an unsatisfying ending for everyone.

If you're hiking somewhere with predators, carry bear spray and please *make sure it's somewhere immediately accessible*. In the scenario that opened the chapter, we perpetually looked like nerdy parents wearing fanny packs with a holster containing bear spray permanently attached to our belts. But had the bear come after Will, it would have been his best chance of survival. Even if you're not in bear country, bear deterrent works effectively against other animals. Most studies say humans (particularly those who aren't well trained in firearms and are beginning outdoors folks, like the audience for this book) are much more likely to be successful with bear spray. As an added bonus, you're encouraging the bear to understand that humans are a pain in the ass.

Stay away from wildlife in general, but especially if they have their chitlins nearby. They can be fiercely protective of their young, and as with humans, you don't want to get into a fight with an angry mama.

Don't camp near a carcass, since a predator may think you're trying to get in on their meal. This seems like an unappetizing thing to avoid anyway, but there are circumstances where it isn't obvious. Several years ago, we hiked into Chicago Basin in southern Colorado, and after a long day that involved getting to camp well after dark, we had *just* set up our tents when we noticed a deer carcass just on the far side of camp. It took all the gumption we had to repack our tent and continue up the trail to the next campsite.

BEARS

To repeat, make sure you have bear spray. Also, hike in groups (this is why some trails in Banff National Park have a minimum requirement of four humans to get a hiking permit in bear-dense areas), as it is extremely rare that a bear will attack a group. When you are out hiking and don't have visibility around a bend or through a forest, talk constantly with your companions. If you run out of things to say, start a song with the basic lyrics of "Hey, bear! Coming through, bear!" You might feel dumb, but you'll feel dumber if you surprise a bear. If you do somehow stumble upon a bear and you are closer than you should be, stay calm. If you run, that bear will also run, and bears always run faster than you. Back away slowly while talking firmly and making yourself as large as possible (for example, open your jacket). If the bear starts to come at you, hold your ground.

There is a substantial difference between grizzly bears and black bears. Black bears are typically more diminutive than grizzlies and are akin to oversize raccoons. Physically, grizzlies have a distinct hump on their shoulder that black bears don't have. Beyond that, your behavior should vary based on which is attacking. If it is a grizz, lay on your stomach and play dead, letting your backpack take the brunt of the force. If it's a black bear, fight back with all you've got (and that bear spray you still have), as these guys will almost always continue attacking until you are D-E-D dead.

WOLVES

Wolf attacks are extremely rare. It is unlikely you'll see one nearby in the wild, much less close enough to be dangerous. If you do find yourself engaged with a wolf, the responsive behavior is very similar to that for bears. Travel in groups, be calm, stand tall, make yourself large, calmly let the animal know that you are not easy prey, and back away slowly. In the remarkably unusual circumstance that the wolf continues to move toward you, deploy the pepper spray and fight back.

HUMP

GRIZZLY
BEAR

VS.

SMALLER

BLACK
BEAR

COUGAR
OR
MOUNTAIN LION
(different names,)
same animal

WOLF

STAY 100 ft.
AWAY

MOUNTAIN LIONS/COUGARS

Fun fact: Those are the same thing (#TheMoreYouKnow). Like wolves, it is relatively rare that you'll see a mountain lion in the wild, although that has changed recently as we continue to encroach on natural mountain lion habitat. The rules of engagement are the same as with bears and wolves: If you are attacked by a cougar, fight back until they leave you alone.

BISON, MOOSE, ELK, MOUNTAIN GOATS, AND OTHER NONPREDATORY SPECIES

If they aren't carnivores, how bad could it be? The simple answer? Disastrous. You don't want to get your ass kicked by a 2,000-pound bison that's essentially a prehistoric animal, and it would be disappointing to be disemboweled by someone with large antlers. Give these animals plenty of room and admire from a distance. If you see someone else trying to pose their child on the back of a bison for a selfie, do the right thing and have your friend video the situation while you calmly try to tell the tourist that they're at great risk for making national news in the worst way possible.

FOOD STORAGE AND MANAGEMENT

If you're in bear country, the answer is simple: Always store food in a bear-proof hard-sided container. We could have an extensive discussion around the merits of hanging food, but the reality is most people are terrible at it doing it properly. Even the ones who are good may not find the perfect arrangement of branches required. Yes, they are a pain in the ass to carry, but at least you get a nice camp seat out of the deal. While we're on the subject, it's not just food that goes inside the bear canister. Store anything with a scent, including sunscreen, adult bum wipes, Sour Patch Kids, and toothpaste.

Also, don't cook near your tent if you can avoid it. Ideally, your camp-site, kitchen area, and food storage are all one hundred yards apart, and the kitchen area is downwind of the other two (as this area usually has the most attractive scent to animals). Be intelligent about the types of food you cook as well. Simmering bacon with some buttery mashed potatoes in an open pan or pot is a wee bit riskier than cooking something in a sealed dehydrated bag. This doesn't mean you get to eat only gorp for a week; make a deliberate assessment about the level of risk you want to take. Personally, we think it makes your first meal back in civilization that much sweeter. Even if you're not in bear country, it is good management to keep any food scents, scraps, or otherwise wildlife-enticing sundries outside your tent. Years ago we were hiking outside of the Maroon Bells, and when we came back to camp our tent was ripped to shreds by (presumably) marmots or other rodents who smelled a bag of food we had absentmindedly left in the tent. It wasn't a life-threatening situation, but we really liked that tent.

CHAPTER ELEVEN

CAMPING WITH KIDS

Read any business book and you'll likely find a consistent recommendation: Find a mentor. This is sound, but it can be difficult to find someone who is willing to invest the interest in offering their wisdom. It takes someone special to willingly give up their hard-earned knowledge, but fortunately, we've found a shortcut: Have a couple of kids. Suddenly you'll find the world has droves of unsolicited advice, and all of it certainly better than whatever cack-handed attempt you made at parenting.

That said, we limit the guidance we offer when it comes to kids. Everyone is different. Just like adults respond differently to life outdoors, so do tiny humans. However, we have found one almost universal truth: Kids are more adaptable and durable than we give them credit for, sometimes even more so than their parents. When our daughter was seven months old we took her on a two-and-a-half-month road trip all over the western United States. We camped in national parks, BLM land, and a couple of proper campgrounds, and during the entire trip, there was only one night when she completely misplaced her fecal matter. (Figuratively, we mean. She literally misplaced it multiple times every day.) Amusingly, it was one of the few nights we couldn't escape, because we were on an island in Channel Islands National Park, so Will walked her around Santa Cruz while she slept on his shoulder. Otherwise, the other seventy-plus nights went smashingly well. She played in the dirt, ate rocks, got a few bug bites and tan toes, and we would do it again in a heartbeat.

Since you're here, you likely *want* advice on how to get your babes into the woods, so we'll offer some additional thoughts. No matter what, don't give up. Some days are better than others, but when you're telling stories to your grandkids about their parents, they'll want to hear about the time you took them to Great Sand Dunes National Park and slept in the dunes, not how they stayed inside and watched *Paw Patrol* so you could have thirty minutes of undivided brainpower to yourself. Although we've done that, too.

When it comes to hiking and/or camping, we think of the kiddos in three categories:

1. **Ones Who Cannot Move Without Assistance (Infants)**
2. **Ones Who Are Mobile Without Any Sense of Self-Preservation (Toddlers)**
3. **Ones Who Are Old Enough to Pretend to Follow Directions and Carry Their Own Stuff (Kids)**

As strange as it sounds at first, hiking with an infant was easiest for us. Liliana slept extremely well in a backpack (it didn't hurt that we had her in there from a very young age), and breastfeeding is an easy way to carry baby food (although we also supplemented). This is a long way of saying start early. It gets much more sporting when they can run.

Once kids can start moving on their own—and they'll want to!—dial back your distances significantly. You always have the option of strapping your child to a kid carrier and letting her hit you in the back of the head for hours on end while she screams, but assuming you want a moderately pleasant experience, give her plenty of time to run around and check out the trail herself. The good news: Eventually she'll tucker out, and you can still cover a few miles while she's in your pack. Also, we'd always recommend bringing a child carrier, even if you think she's going to walk the whole way. Schlepping a twenty-five-pound kid in your arms works around the house, but it's a heck of a workout if you're trying to cover a couple of miles on the trail.

At some point they will finally reach the age when they can carry their own stuff, which is generally around age five. At this point, kids can be in significantly different stages of their hiking comfort and development, so the answer is simple: Start small with trips that have a high ratio of child-

fun to pain, and then progress at a pace the whole family can handle. Remember, your offspring may find a talus field significantly more fun than a summit, much in the same way they loved reading *Green Eggs and Ham* one hundred times in a single night and you wanted to vomit.

Regardless of development, here are a few things we learned that apply at any age.

BE OPTIMISTIC, BUT SET REASONABLE EXPECTATIONS

You've likely read that happiness equals reality minus expectations, and that could not be truer than when sleeping in a tent with your little nugget. We generally like to set our expectations at "No one died," which has been key to ensuring happiness on every trip. Also, we scaled slowly. Our first night we tested car camping in Utah just outside of Capitol Reef National Park. After a few more successful sessions, we graduated to a single overnight in Sedona, Arizona. We hiked only a couple of miles with our packs and we were gone less than twenty-four hours, but watching the sunrise from our perch on Brin's Mesa is easily one of our favorite memories as a family. Plus, once you overnight with a kid, it's very easy to extend it to multiple nights. All you are doing is carrying a few more diapers, extra food, and tiny little kid's clothes.

Also, at the risk of being obvious, it is much easier to camp in warmer climates than cold. Technically, our first overnight was a backcountry ski trip to the Maroon Hut outside of Crested Butte, Colorado. It is a relatively easy ski in, but Liliana was four months old and still breastfeeding. About an hour short of the hut we had to pull over to feed her. One small catch: It was five degrees in a late-February snowstorm. Thankfully, Heather is a badass mama (Will's words, for clarification) and tucked Liliana inside her jacket so she could breastfeed her nestled in her own cocoon. In the spirit of maintaining optimism, it was preferable to dealing with one of those how-did-you-get-poop-on-the-back-of-your-neck blowouts.

FIND FRIENDS

After our first successful overnight on Brin's Mesa, we went all-in a month later with a five-day trip to Will's favorite place on the planet, the Ansel Adams Wilderness. This abuts the southeastern side of Yosemite, and it's quintessential Sierra, with its alpine lakes, granite peaks, and perfect summer days. But including our cherub, there was an extra forty pounds of weight that we normally don't need to worry about. This is where our friends came in. The three extra folks each picked up about ten pounds of gear (one of them doubled to twenty when he carried out all the dirty diapers), and we'll certainly repay the favor if they ever bother to have kids of their own. The point is, ask for help. Most people are thankful for the opportunity to be a part of your post-children outdoor lifestyle, and we've found many of our friends are inspired when they see it can actually happen.

This trip was also an excellent example of setting reasonable expectations. Normally we'd hike from the trailhead to Thousand Island Lake (about eight miles) in a single day, but instead we did it in two. Shorter days are good for obvious reasons, but it also meant we camped alongside Gem Lake, a place we'd hurriedly skipped past on previous trips to the same area. It was absolute magic, and Liliana splashed in the lake for hours because we arrived early enough in the day to actually enjoy it. That's a Michael Scott win-win-win.

JUST LIKE GROWN-ASS ADULTS, THEY'LL BE MISERABLE WHEN THEY'RE WET, COLD, AND/OR HUNGRY

The difference is you must proactively stay ahead of it, especially when their communication skills are limited to different octaves and decibel levels of very loud noises. It's easy to get into the zone when hiking, so build a schedule and stick to it. Feed them consistently, and every hour

(or whatever works for you), take a minute to have someone else in your group check and make sure they aren't getting cold *or* hot. Many parents (us included) have been guilty of overdressing their kids, and it is only after an hour or two on the trail that we realize we accidentally put our kid in a Bikram hiking class. And for the love of everything outdoor, change their diaper routinely (probably more often than at home, and especially in hot and humid environments). Imagine you hiked ten miles in jeans, earned yourself some wicked chafing on your inner thighs, and then had to go ride a camel. That's the equivalent of what happens to a kid with diaper rash in one of the kid-carry packs.

GEAR

If you're looking for an excuse to spend more money on outdoors gear, your wish is granted. This isn't intended to be an exhaustive list (for example, don't forget wipes, as they are a little bit of bliss for adults, too), but it reveals some key things we've learned.

Tents: On our first overnight we squeezed into a twenty-eight-square-foot two-person tent, and Will shared a twenty-five-inch-wide pad with Liliana while Heather mashed her face against the opposite nylon wall. Cozy, no? The lesson: Even though she is only an eighth of our size, assume she'll consume at least one-third of the space. As a bonus, tents are like padded romper rooms for toddlers. Generally there's nothing but puffy sleeping bags, air-filled mattresses, nylon walls, and two adults who are happy to not worry about their offspring going dome-first into the corner of a coffee table.

Sleeping Bags and Pads: As alluded to above, acquire one sleeping pad per human if you're backpacking. We put Liliana in a down-insulated snowsuit and Will then slept with an extra-wide down quilt that he used to cover both him and Liliana. In the morning, Heather would pull Liliana into her bag and use the same quilt as a makeshift blackout curtain in the hopes of keeping the boisterous baby in bed later than five a.m. If you are car camping, find an extra-wide two-person sleeping bag setup and put your babe in the middle. (We put her on a Dock-a-Tot when she was really young to ensure we didn't smoosh her.) We successfully slept several nights with twenty-degree temps outside of Bryce Canyon, and Liliana never got that cold because Will snuggled with her all night, creating one of his favorite memories as a dad.

Child Carriers: When they are really young, have one parent stash them in a front carry while they also cart a lightweight backpack. This method also works really well for cold weather. When we visited the aforementioned Maroon Hut in Crested Butte, Heather carried Liliana into the hut in subfreezing temps while she slept the entire way, warmly cocooned against her body (while Will carted absolutely everything else). Once they get a little older you'll likely transfer to a backpack-style carry. Make sure you test several, as we had different brands feel fine in the store before grinding our hips into bloody submission when they were fully loaded out on the trail. (Heather still has the scars to prove it.) Make sure there's a way to easily carry a water bladder, and we strongly recommend grabbing one with an integrated sun shade. It helps to have a large cargo pocket as well. Even if you're not as loaded as normal because you're responsible for being somewhat nimble with a kid strapped to your back, it helps to have space for high-volume, lightweight goods like unused diapers, puffy jackets, and other items of similar ilk.

START EARLY AND MAKE IT A HABIT

This goes for you more than it goes for the kid. The kid will adapt to whatever you set as normal; what is important is that *you* mentally adjust to the massive change to your outdoor lifestyle. As soon as everyone is feeling healthy, start putting outdoor adventures on the calendar every other month and get out there. Don't overdo it; even little overnight trips with your friends will go a long way to making habits like sleeping in a tent as easy as possible.

Bottom line: The outdoors are good for your progeny, and they're good for your family, too. Clearly we are outdoorsy folks, so this is said

with great bias, but we are the best versions of ourselves when we are outside together. There's no living room to pick up, no laundry to fold, no Legos to step on, just unadulterated family time. Every night when baby girl goes to sleep, we parents get a few hours of one-on-one time without a single distraction (other than the occasional shooting star). It's romantic, fulfilling, and an important part of who we are as a couple and family.

CHAPTER TWELVE

CAMPING AND HIKING ON A BUDGET

On his first-ever overnight backpacking trip outside of Sedona, Will carried four gallons of water (amounting to ten pounds when you add in the weight of the hard-sided containers) rather than spend seventy bucks on a twelve-ounce water filter. On Heather's first trip, she carried several pounds of canned meat and soups because it was cheaper than dehydrated meals (and, admittedly, she wasn't really into cooking). She wore a sweatshirt from her old college dance team and wore khaki-colored shorts that looked outdoorsy but actually came from Old Navy.

The point is this: Camping is the original dirtbag pastime (and in these echelons, *dirtbag* is a hallowed moniker). Modern hiking ethos and a desire to not starve may change your approach when compared to iconic outdoorists of the past, but it is a good reminder that not *everything*

needs to be pulled from a catalog page of your favorite retailer. Assuming you've covered the basics required for safety, spending above and beyond is largely a function of desired comfort, usually measured in the amount of weight you're carrying on your back. You'll have to decide for yourself: How many dollars do you want to save by carrying a heavier load?

GEAR

If you're headed out for a backpacking trip, there are a few items we recommend not scrimping on too much: footwear and packs, followed closely by shelter. You'll ask a lot of your feet, so you want something that is durable enough to handle the abuse, as well as strong enough to support the extra load on your back. Your urban running shoes are likely not the answer. Current trends frequently put people in low-cut (and lighter) trail runners, but we'd recommend starting with a more traditional pair of high ankle boots. Aside from the obvious ankle protection and support, they will also last you through more seasons if you decide to push your hiking into early spring or late autumn. As far as packs go, there are plenty of durable, hiking-specific packs that will carry a large load relatively well. The pack itself will be heavy, but it is more important that it has the hip belts, back stays, and similar elements that transfer weight to your body in a healthy way. Finally, heavy tents are just fine, but don't procure something that isn't designed to handle inclement weather. If everything else goes sideways and you end up in your tent for a weekend, that's okay as long as you stay warm and dry (and that could be quite romantic, depending on your company).

Otherwise, you can frequently cobble together the rest of your kit from what is already around the house. For example, your kitchen cutlery works just fine, and if you're looking for a camp bowl you can use a resealable plastic container. Headlamps are convenient because they're hands-free, but a flashlight will work well too.

If you are headed out for a car camping trip, there's a chance you won't need to buy anything new at all. Start with a warm summer trip and all you need are a couple of blankets, some food out of your pantry and fridge, and some gumption to ignore the bugs that may crawl into bed with you. Most weather forecasts are accurate enough that rain shouldn't sneak up on you, but if it does, you can hop in the car and you'll survive the night just fine.

eBay is a great spot to find used gear. If you are old-school, you may prefer brick and mortar to e-comm, so check your local outdoor retailers for used-gear sales. Back near the turn of the century, Will would organize quarterly events at the REI Garage Sale, where he and fifteen of his outdoor friends would spend the night in the REI parking lot so they could be first in line when the doors opened the next morning. (Yet another reason Heather is glad she didn't meet her husband until well into their

GEAR

SPEND

SAVE

adulthood!) Here are a few other spots you can make trades when it comes to buying gear:

Sleeping Bags: Synthetic bags are generally less expensive than down bags. If you buy a used one, make sure it's not so old that it has lost its ability to insulate. Down bags will generally regain their loft when you clean them, but synthetics are much less likely to do so.

Sleeping Pads: Closed-cell sleeping pads are inexpensive and never pop. They may not be as girthy as their air-filled counterparts, but you can use two of them if that really matters to you.

Rainwear: Many people will get rid of quality rain gear after a couple of seasons because it no longer seems waterproof. It's likely the water-proof finish wore off. Buy the used garment, put it through the wash with some aftermarket durable water repellant (DWR), and it will likely be good as new.

Stoves: The newfangled canister stoves are delightfully efficient, but a thirty-dollar canister stove and a single pot to boil water can get a hiker through most weekend meals just fine.

DESTINATIONS

We have a German family friend who visited California in the late seventies, and based on popular media and general expectations, he assumed he'd spend two weeks sleeping anywhere he wanted on the beach with a free-living collection of bronzed Left Coast denizens. Lamentably, that was not the case, and he found out the hard way that not all camping (even on public lands!) is free. If it is public land, why are you getting charged to sleep on a patch of dirt?

The answer, of course, is location and amenities. Thankfully, there are plenty of alternatives, and we rarely camp in formal campgrounds even when we're car camping. You simply need to understand how public lands work. We generally look for National Forest and/or BLM land, as they mostly do not have camping restrictions. Of course, you'll need to be self-sufficient, so we load up the back of the truck with a cooler (it is less expensive to buy regular groceries than specialized backpacking food anyway) and head out to our free campsite. With National Forest territory in particular, you can frequently find Off-Highway Vehicle (OHV) maps with free recommended campsites. We stumbled upon one of our favorites in Northern Colorado entirely by accident, and it's still a classic spot to this day. Don't dismiss the power of a good ol' map.

Google Earth is also an excellent resource. Find public lands that have an open camping policy, and then cruise the terrain at home looking for flat campsites in hard-to-find places. You can also use this to do research on backcountry zones that are off the beaten path. For example, Colorado's fourteeners are perpetually popular, but thirteeners (peaks over 13,000 feet) frequently have adventurous hikes to the summit with unmitigated views from the top. To be sure, data on thirteeners is tougher to find. But, if we want a fun summit hike, we can easily use Google Earth and find a free campsite at the base of a peak where we can set up our base camp for summit day.

However, there is a good reason the National Park Service is the crown jewel of our public lands, so here is some advice on how to visit these parks on a budget. To start, many national parks have national forests or similar public lands that surround the primary park. When we visited Capitol Reef National Park with our nine-month-old daughter, we camped in BLM land to the east of the park. We certainly enjoyed the privacy of having no one near our tent for a half-mile, which we were doubly thankful for when she embarked upon unadulterated happy squealing at 5:15 a.m. when she realized she was inside her favorite fort. We also camped in Dixie National Forest when we visited Bryce Canyon and Kaibab National Forest when we visited the Grand Canyon. In each location we had a private campsite, and in the Grand Canyon there was even a trailhead within a half-mile of our campsite that we could follow to the north rim of the Grand Canyon. We got up early each day to get into the park before the crowds, and we scored prime parking spots at each location where we set up shop for the day.

CAMPSITE BUDGET OPTIONS
13ERS
NATIONAL FORESTS
BACKCOUNTRY ZONES
PUBLIC LANDS
BLM
BEAUTIFUL
National Park
FULL OF AMENITIES AND PEOPLE

Also, don't forget to pack your own food ahead of time. Unlike the movie theaters, rangers won't check your bags to see if you're bringing in your own box of Whoppers, so load up the cooler and bring everything you need in your vehicle. Frequently, if you get in early you can find a parking spot right next to a picnic table with a view, and you'll be the envy of all your new neighbors when you break out your lunch in lieu of shelling out twelve bucks for a tub of fries.

The final note on national parks: Although the campgrounds can be expensive and crowded, typically the backcountry sites are free or inex-

pensive, and you can still feel like you have the place to yourself. Start simple: Camp outside the park on Friday, then head in early on Saturday for a quick overnight. Even if your pack is heavy, you can make it far enough down the trail to avoid the crowds, as many people won't hike more than a mile or two from the parking lot.

CHAPTER THIRTEEN

CAMPING IN NATIONAL PARKS

***According to Ken Burns, the National Park Service is "America's Best Idea,"
and we understand the sentiment.*** The
National Park Service operates fifty-eight different parks throughout
the United States, and each one is unique and beautiful in its own right.
Want purple mountains and their majesty? Head to Rocky Mountain
National Park in Colorado. Prefer gigantic trees so girthy that you can
drive your car through them? Try California's Sequoia National Park.
Are you more interested in fierce-looking gators and swampy marshes?
Florida's Everglades National Park is the place for you.

Camping in national parks can be great fun, but it is different from other places. There are rules and regulations in place that are important to know before venturing out on that park-heavy road trip. After all, who wants to wake up to a ranger shining a light in your face at two in the morning because he found you sleeping on the side of the road? (We swear, it could've happened to anyone.)

WHERE CAMPING IS AND IS NOT ALLOWED

Let's start here, because it feels like a great idea to identify where you are allowed to sleep to avoid that aforementioned ranger incident. In national parks, campers typically have two options: frontcountry campgrounds and backcountry campsites.

FRONTCOUNTRY CAMPGROUNDS

Frontcountry camping in national parks is easily the most popular option with Americans who want the relative ease and comfort of park campgrounds. Most national parks have at least one or two established campgrounds with roads shaped in loops. Multiple campsites line the roads, with certain areas specific to tent camping and others for RV camping. (You have to separate the two to avoid inner-camp battles over whose generator is louder. We're talking *Game of Thrones* levels of ferocity here.)

Most of these campgrounds have similar amenities that make them great for beginner campers and those who want a few creature comforts. There is always some type of check-in station where you pay and get a tag that identifies your campsite number and how long you are staying. The latter point becomes especially important in popular campgrounds where drop-in camping is an option. Have you ever seen sharks circling? It's like that, times a billion.

There is usually a parking spot for one or two vehicles, and potable water is available throughout the campgrounds. Bathrooms are dispersed through the area as well, and some campgrounds even have showers. If you opt for an RV site, there will be an electrical hookup along with a dump station to throw out your dirty water. Picnic tables are standard, along with established fire rings for campfires. Most national park campgrounds even have camp stores to buy luxuries (ahem, MARSHMALLOWS) and bundles of firewood. If you're camping in an area rife with wildlife, each campsite will likely include a food storage bin, as well.

BACKCOUNTRY CAMPSITES

If you are feeling adventurous, traveling the backcountry of a national park can be one of the best ways to get off the beaten path and explore scenic areas that many people never get to see. Unlike the frontcountry campgrounds, there won't be a lot of amenities . . . or really any, unless you include fresh air and a live sound machine complete with options for wind whistling in the trees, water babbling in the creek, and birds chirp-

WELCOME TO YOUR CAMPGROUND!

~KEY~

- - - Pathway
- Road
- 1,2,3...Campsite
- Bathroom
- Ranger Station
- Makeout Spot
- Camp Store
- Parking
- Kids' Fort
- RV Site
- Drinking Water
- Recycling
- Bird Blind
- Shower
- Hidden S'mores
- Playground
- Picnic Area
- Whiskey Cave

ing good morning (#WorthIt). But the trade-off is that you will likely get solitude, peace, and maybe even morning coffee with a few of your favorite furry friends.

One word to the wise: Just because you are camping in the backcountry doesn't mean you can go all willy-nilly and ignore the rules. Frequently, the backcountry sites in national parks require permits, so do your research before the trip. In popular parks such as Yosemite National Park, there is a great chance you'll need to nab your permits months in advance. In quieter locations such as Great Sand Dunes National Park in Colorado, you show up thirty minutes before the permit window opens up for that day. Don't be a noob: Know before you go.

THE COST OF CAMPING

If you have a Magic 8 Ball on you, give it a good shake and it will tell you "All Signs Point to Yes." Camping—both frontcountry and backcountry—is not free in national parks, which is why it typically isn't listed on any budget-minded camping list.

We know, we know. But, think about all of the good your campsite fee is bringing to the park! Those funds help pay the park rangers' salaries, provide the frontcountry amenities that you may enjoy, and maintain roads and trails and bathrooms. When you think about it, we truly are lucky to have such beautiful land for recreation. We think it's well worth the money to know that we are helping protect these areas for future generations (and our kid thinks so, too). The fees vary from park to park, and frontcountry campsites typically cost more than backcountry sites. Prices also fluctuate from year to year, but campsites usually run from twenty to thirty dollars per night. And don't forget: You need to pay a fee to gain entrance to the park, too.

MAKING RESERVATIONS FOR CAMPSITES

Speaking in generalities is never a good idea, or so says Heather's high school English teacher, but let's break that cardinal rule and hope Mrs. Babb doesn't come back to get us later. In general, yes, you should always make a reservation to camp at a national park.

National parks are popular locations, especially in the summer when kids are out of school and families go on vacation. These protected areas house some of the most beautiful land in the country, so it makes sense that so many people want to visit. But it sure would be a bummer to plan out an entire trip only to show up and realize that your mortal enemy nabbed the last campsite and will be enjoying s'mores under a glittering sky while you're fifty miles away in a dingy hotel room with a bathroom toilet that makes you jiggle the handle and a faucet that consistently drips. You know?

Again, the popularity and need for reservations varies from park to park. Yellowstone National Park in Wyoming and Zion National Park in Utah are prime examples of parks where advance reservations are not only a good idea, but a necessity. In those places, no reservation likely means no camping, which would be totally lame.

DOG RULES IN PARKS

Camping with Fido can be a joy but also quite tricky, especially in national parks. The rules vary from park to park: Some parks do not allow pets at all, while others allow pets in developed areas like campgrounds. Some trails allow dogs while others do not, but they are almost always forbidden in the backcountry and at backcountry campsites. When they are allowed, dogs are required to be on a leash not exceeding six feet in length and never, ever off-leash. The requirements vary widely, so once you've established your itinerary, peruse the website for your chosen national park and read up on their pet policy. That will help you decide whether Fido rides along or stays behind with Grandma.

OUR FAVORITE NATIONAL PARKS FOR CAMPING

Drumroll, please! If you've made it this far in the chapter, we realize that is likely because you are here for only one thing: Which national parks have the best camping? And really, that is an unfair question. That is like asking us to choose which of our children is our favorite. (Which actually isn't that difficult since we have only one and she would be highly offended if we opted for another kid. But still, our point stands.)

Camping in national parks is as subjective as your political views, but these are our ten favorite campgrounds in no particular order.

1. **Piñon Flats, Great Sand Dunes National Park, Colorado**
2. **Camp 4, Yosemite National Park, California**
3. **Slough Creek Campground, Yosemite National Park, Wyoming**
4. **Wonder Lake Campground, Denali National Park, Alaska**
5. **North Rim Campground, Grand Canyon National Park, Arizona**
6. **Namakanipaio Campground, Hawaii Volcanoes National Park, Hawaii**
7. **Scorpion Ranch Campground, Santa Cruz Island, Channel Islands National Park, California**
8. **Gulpha Gorge Campground, Hot Springs National Park, Arkansas**
9. **Assateague Island, Assateague Island National Seashore, Maryland**
10. **Mathews Arm Campground, Shenandoah National Park, Virginia**

TOP TEN NATIONAL

PIÑON FLATS
GREAT SAND DUNES NAT'L PARK, CO

CAMP 4
YOSEMITE, CA

SLOUGH CREEK
YELLOWSTONE, WY

WONDER LAKE CAMPGROUND
DENALI, AL

NORTH RIM
GRAND CANYON, AZ

PARK CAMPGROUNDS

SCORPION RANCH CAMPGROUND

CHANNEL ISLANDS, CA

NAMAKANIPAIO

HAWAII VOLCANOES, BIG ISLAND, HI

GULPHA GORGE

HOT SPRINGS, AZ

ASSATEAGUE ISLAND

NATIONAL SEASHORE, MD

MATHEWS ARM

SHENANDOAH, VA

CHAPTER FOURTEEN

BACKYARD CAMPING

We're going to do you a huge solid right now: Slowly back away from the disorganized pile of camping gear and put down the dusty bin of plastic dishes from your last camping trip that likely need to be washed. Do you see a chair somewhere? Sit in it. And put away your phone, too, so you won't be tempted to do any campground research or Amazon shopping for last-minute gear items you know you don't have. Take three deep breaths and relax. Don't you feel better now?

So frequently, we forget that camping is about enjoyment and family time. It can be hard to remember this when you are wrapped up in the organization and planning of your trip, mapping distances with your atlas, and scrimping and saving to afford all of the campground and park entry fees. At its core, camping is a return to your roots, to Mother Nature, and to those you love. And, fun fact: You can do it anywhere. That's why backyard camping is so darn awesome.

WHAT IS BACKYARD CAMPING?

Since it's so aptly named, we're willing to bet that you've got this definition dialed. Backyard camping is exactly what it sounds like: camping out in your backyard (or front yard) or even your living room. Anywhere on your property, or even in the general vicinity, will work, since the idea is to stay close to home. This means you get the benefits of spending time with each other outside without all of the hassle and stress of planning for a larger camping adventure. Sounds pretty good, right?

Backyard camping can be a great option for so many reasons. For a young family nervous to dive into the deep end of the proverbial patch of dirt, backyard camping is a great entry point. You can help your children adjust to tent life without the pressure and pandemonium of a new location. If the poop hits the fan and your kiddo wakes up at two a.m. wailing because she needs her favorite dinosaur-shaped night-light and the sleeping bag is slippery and her pillow lost air and where is Puffy the Panda, it is simple enough to gather up the distressed daughter and take her in the house where she will be more comfortable. It is an easy escape plan, and it is one that makes new families significantly more comfortable (#Winning).

You know who else loves backyard camping? You. Well, we think you do, especially if you are someone who is new to camping and/or has some shiny new gear without a ton of experience. Once upon a time, Heather was a college student who decided a grand adventure to Moab would be a great idea. Because she and her friends were nineteen and clearly invincible, they waited until after work on Friday evening to begin the five-hour drive to Utah. They pulled into the outskirts of town around three in the morning, unsure of where to camp and even less sure about the new tent packed in the back of the car. After fumbling with the contraption for a solid thirty-four minutes and twenty-two seconds, she and her friends called an audible after snapping a pole like a twig. Exhausted and frustrated, they threw the whole thing in the back seat of the car (bucket of sand included) and passed out in the dirt. They awoke at dawn to realize two things: They had ruined their new tent, and they were sleeping five feet from a construction site. Don't be like Heather: Test your new gear in a controlled environment, like backyard camping.

TIPS FOR BACKYARD CAMPING

Of course, backyard camping still takes some prep work, especially if you want to make it a memorable evening for your family. (Or your best friend or your dog. We don't judge.) Below are some of our favorite tips for creating a successful night of camping under the stars . . . and maybe under your back deck.

CREATE A COZY SLEEPING SPACE

For backpacking, you are looking at bare bones: the lightest, the smallest, and the most portable. On the flip side, you don't need to worry about any of that when you are sleeping twenty feet from your house. Bring a tent outside, of course, but don't be afraid to liven this party up to create a fun atmosphere. If you have any battery-operated twinkle lights, those are always a hit, especially for small children who get uncomfortable in the dark. If you think your spine would prefer to stay away from the ultralight sleeping pad you acquired for your thirty-five-mile hiking adventure, don't be afraid to use that gigantic air mattress tucked away in your guest room closet. Heck, you can even lug the vacuum outside to inflate it, if needed. We won't tell. The point is to create a comfortable fortress of sorts so that everyone has a good time—and wants to do it again soon.

If you don't own a tent but want to get outside, there are still options, so don't give up hope! If you have older kids or a confident BFF, feel free to cowboy camp. Lay down that air mattress in the grass, pile the blankets on top, and cross your fingers that it doesn't rain. If your family prefers a bit more coverage, string up a clothesline and throw a tarp or blanket over the top. Voilà! You've got yourself a cozy A-frame shelter that is perfect for your backyard evening.

PLAY LOTS OF GAMES

When you are camping at a campground, there is plenty to entertain: campfires, camp activities, nature sounds, and other people. But just because you are camping in the yard doesn't mean you need to let go of that sense of wonder. Create activities that will keep your family entertained from the late afternoon into the evening. Take a hike around the neighborhood and bring your binoculars and camera, just like you would in the mountains. Ask your children to snap photos of anything fun or weird they see, and review them later in the tent. (Carefully yet quickly delete those photos your daughter accidentally snapped of your naked neigh-

bor. Trust us — it's better for everyone if those go away.) At dusk, hide a fun object (like maybe the bag of s'mores fixings) somewhere in the yard and challenge the kiddos to find it using only their flashlights or headlamps. Of course, the reward is the sweet dessert. But as anyone who has ever spent six hours hunting for Easter eggs can attest, the search is half the fun. After dark, climb into the tent and share stories — ghostly or not, depending on the crowd — until no one can keep their eyes open any longer. As for bedtime? Don't bother. Backyard camping is a special treat; everyday rules can wait till morning.

DON'T FORGET THE FOOD

There is a great chance you won't have a campfire in your backyard (and if you do, maybe look into the laws and regulations before the fire department shows up and ruins your entire evening. We can't think of a worse way to welcome the new neighbor to your 'hood than setting his house on fire. Just saying). But, you can still create camping meals by using a grill. Hot dogs and baked beans are easy to cook, and they evoke a wonderful feeling of Americana camping. Pre-cut some veggies like peppers and zucchini and onions and wrap those in foil before chucking it all on the grill. Or, if you want to keep it über-simple, make a gigantic pot of stew beforehand and warm it up while the kids are playing. All of these options are easy, which means you have plenty of time to focus on the priorities, like dessert. Pro tip: Making s'mores on a grill isn't as easy as it looks, but buying one of those s'mores makers at Walmart or Target makes you the hero. Then, you just create your s'mores sandwiches like usual, place them in the handy gadget, and warm them over the grill's heat. It may not have the same romantic feeling as campfire s'mores, but we don't think your children will care after they're five marshmallows deep with chocolate oozing down their chins.

STAY OUTSIDE THE ENTIRE TIME

Half of the fun of backyard camping is making it feel like a grander camping adventure, so don't ruin the atmosphere by heading inside every five minutes to grab something you forgot or to check your phone or to an-

swer the front door. Once you and your family are outside, stay outside. And once you climb into the tent for the night, stay in the tent (unless someone has to pee, in which case you guys can make the call as to whether you want to advocate peeing on the fence line or breaking the outside rule). The point is to enjoy a pseudo-camping adventure, so try your absolute best to stay outside until the birds begin chirping the following day.

CHAPTER FIFTEEN

CAMPING RESPONSIBLY

Unless you're living under a rock, you've heard of Instagram. If you're hip to the game, you probably have an account yourself so you can double tap all of the astronomically beautiful locations, so pristine and perfect that they practically appear fake.

News flash: Don't believe everything you see on the internet.

Take those photos with a grain of salt. Believe it or not, there are a lot of people in the world who will set up staged photos just to capture that beautiful Insta-moment. And while they sure look good, they are often Insta-irresponsible and Insta-damaging to the environment.

Think back to your Instagram scrolling and consider the following. How many times have you seen a photo of a tent precariously perched on the edge of a cliff with rocks practically sliding down to the valley floor? Or pitched five feet from a pristine alpine lake to snag those sunset views? Or an avid hiker lounging in a field full of wildflowers, blooms surrounding her smiling face while she enjoys Mother Nature's bounty? If you're anything like us, you see it all the time, and it makes you cringe more than your grandmother singing "My Heart Will Go On" at Friday-night karaoke.

But hold up: How can camping damage the environment? Isn't that reserved for those who charter private jets and dump truckloads of trash into the ocean and throw soda cans out their car window and hate babies?

Camping responsibly is a concept that leaped into the limelight in recent years, thanks in large part to the efforts of a nonprofit known as the Leave No Trace Center for Outdoor Ethics. Leave No Trace (LNT) is an outdoor program dedicated to educating and inspiring people to get outside on the trail and in tents in a responsible fashion. Because that's the thing: Your neighbor running around carving his name into tree trunks might not know any better. (Let's give him the benefit of the doubt, okay?)

At the core of LNT lie seven principles that act as the bedrock for all responsible activity in the outdoors. When camping, it's a good idea to consider these seven principles when making your decisions. If something doesn't align? Maybe it's not your best choice.

PLAN AHEAD AND PREPARE

I mean, duh. It almost sounds too simple, right? Of course you'll plan ahead for your camping trip, right? But it turns out that planning ahead can help aid LNT in more ways than you may initially realize. For example, sit down and take the time to look into the regulations and policies of the

area where you will be camping. Maybe campfires are usually allowed but are banned from July through August because of fire season? That's good to know ahead of time, since Smokey Bear says only you can prevent forest fires. It's also a great idea to sit down and look at the size of the group you will be camping with. Smaller groups inherently leave a smaller impact on the environment (and on your personal whiskey stash), so try to plan trips with fewer people. If you are wildly popular and have more than a thousand followers on Instagram, consider planning two trips over the summer to break up the number of people and do Mother Nature a huge solid.

Backpackers have different factors to consider. Waste in the backcountry is not as easy to get to a trash can (more on this later), so it's über-helpful to have less trash. Lay out all of your food ahead of time and evaluate where you can consolidate. Pack your eggs in a multiple-use container (purchased at any outdoor goods store) rather than schlepping in the egg carton that becomes trash when breakfast is over. Bring reusable water bottles and bladders instead of single-use plastic options. Not only will these make your trip less messy, but it's a heckuva lot better for our planet.

TRAVEL AND CAMP ON DURABLE SURFACES

Let's go back to that picture-perfect Instagram photo with the tent perched next to the alpine lake. Guess what: zero points. Ideally, campers should always look for the most durable and/or established surface possible to pitch their tent and set up camp. Usually, this means surfaces of gravel, dirt, rock, dry grasses, or even snow (although if you're camping in the snow, you likely don't need our help!). If you see an established campsite, use that. If you're camping in a pristine area, spread out to avoid creating identifiable campsites.

Now for the bad news: LNT suggests always camping at least two hundred feet from lakes and streams. This protects riparian areas from all the

200 FeeT

human gunk that could rinse into the water and affect aquatic life. After all, just because you ate a donut for breakfast doesn't mean a bottom-feeder catfish should enjoy a Krispy Kreme.

When in doubt, consider this: Good campsites are found, not made. If you have to chop down branches, trample shrubs, or move a beehive, make it easy on yourself and look elsewhere.

DISPOSE OF WASTE PROPERLY

Let's say it together: Poop. Poop, poop, poop.

Now that we've gotten that out of the way, let's talk about what to do with your poop while camping. This is arguably one of the touchiest and most sensitive topics to those first adventuring into the outdoors. We can't tell you how many times our friends have looked at us in panic, sheer

terror in their eyes while asking, "But what do I do if I have to go to the bathroom?"

You go. No problem. Just handle it properly.

First, find an appropriate place to poop. We're willing to bet that won't be in the middle of your campsite or smack dab on the trail, right? It should also be at least two hundred feet from water (because, ewwww, gross) and the trail (because no one wants to stumble on that mess). Once you've chosen your backcountry throne, use a small trowel to dig a hole that is six to eight inches deep. Poop into that, and then cover it back up when you're finished. Always pack out your used toilet paper, and definitely don't get clever by trying to burn it. That is an old-school method of dealing with used TP, but it's obvi a terrible idea (please, see Smokey the Bear reference above). Instead, pack it into a Ziploc bag and dispose of it at the trailhead when you get back to the car.

In terms of general food waste, it's pretty basic: If you pack it in, pack it out. Don't dump food scraps in the woods or empty your coffee on a flower because it isn't a Starbucks Venti Half-Caf Soy Latte at precisely 120 degrees. Animals will eat anything you chuck into the woods, and they clearly aren't meant to live life caffeinated. Save them from themselves (and the insane caffeine high they will later achieve) and either consume or pack out all of your trash and food scraps.

LEAVE WHAT YOU FIND

Remember when you were in kindergarten and your teacher told you to look but not touch? She was likely referencing that other kid's peanut butter and jelly sandwich, but the same rule applies here.

One of the coolest things about camping is seeing the beauty created by Mother Nature. She compiled mind-boggling arrangements like dusky orange flowers loaded with petals and towering rock structures with tiny attachments that look like they're going to tip at any moment. As tempting as it may be to touch and explore these things with your hands (or even take one home as a souvenir), please don't. Try your best to keep your hands to yourself so that others can enjoy what you see just as you see it.

And for the love, if you come across historic relics like pottery or arrowheads, do not pass go, do not collect one hundred dollars, and do not put it in your pocket.

MINIMIZE CAMPFIRE IMPACTS

We touched on this in chapter 5, but now we've got time to take a deep dive into the topic. Look, we totally get it: Campfires are the quintessential symbol of Americana camping, and we even once had a friend threaten to throw himself into the lake if he couldn't have a fire (don't worry, he can swim). The licking flames, roaring sparks, and melting s'mores trigger a Pavlovian response that almost immediately calls for you to snuggle up in a camp chair and sing "Kumbaya."

Actually, now that we think about it, that's another great reason to avoid campfires—no "Kumbaya."

But in all seriousness, backcountry campfires ideally should be restricted to emergency situations. The heat causes lasting impacts to the environment, especially in fragile ecosystems such as the high alpine, where vegetation is significantly slower to recover. Plus, consider what you are burning to achieve that fire. If you packed a bundle of wood twelve miles up the mountain, good on you; have you considered *American Ninja Warrior*? But more likely, you're gathering downed wood from the surrounding area. Interestingly enough, this wood contains most of the nitrogen, phosphorous, and potassium that goes back into the soil. You wouldn't want to burn the soil's nitrogen, would you? Carry a backpacking stove and enjoy the fact that your jacket won't smell like smoke for the rest of eternity.

Now, if you're camping in a frontcountry campground or dispersed campsite with clearly established fire rings, have at it. Bring your own wood so you aren't scavenging from the surrounding areas (kindling is okay), and don't forget to pack the Reese's Peanut Butter Cups. After all, everyone knows those make the best s'mores.

RESPECT WILDLIFE

Once upon a time, there was a well-intentioned but naïve family who made the national news when they came upon a baby bison in Yellowstone National Park. It was somewhat chilly and the calf wasn't wearing his winter parka or snow boots, so the family thought they'd do him a huge favor. They loaded the baby bison into the back of their car so he could stay warm while they drove him to the ranger's station.

But seriously.

Sadly, the baby bison was euthanized because its mother later rejected him because of "human interference." Sure, it's an extreme case, but one worth noting since it proves our point: Humans should respect wildlife. When camping, try to keep your distance. It may be tempting to line up next to a deer to see who can clear the fence faster, but it isn't doing them any favors (plus, you're going to lose every time). Feeding animals also earns you zero points, even if they walk right up to your camp and hold out their little hoof-hands. In fact, sometimes you may have to put in concerted effort to avoid feeding them. In Colorado's Chicago Basin, the local mountain goats have an absurd (and sodium-intense) infatuation with human urine. Like, you'll be peeing on a rock and turn around to find a mountain goat four inches from your backside, his tongue wagging in excitement as he tries to knock you out of the way in an effort to get to the good (yellow) stuff. Of course, while they're there, the goats absolutely will try to swing through camp and have a taste of your beef stroganoff too. After all, what goes better with urine aside from stroganoff? Regardless of their Herculean efforts, keep your food away from wildlife by protecting it and storing it in animal-safe containers such as bear canisters or bear bags.

And if you know you're camping in an area where animals are mating or nesting or otherwise sensitive? Tread lightly. There is nothing more terrifying than a massive moose who thinks you are the main problem standing between her and her baby.

BE CONSIDERATE OF OTHER VISITORS

Hey, guess what: This last principle isn't about the environment. Instead, we're considering other people. You know, those humans who will likely share campgrounds or hiking trails with you somewhat routinely. We're all camping to get out of the city and enjoy the sights and sounds of our wild spaces, right? Don't be an ass-hat by blasting your music so loudly that people on the other side of the campground can hear your Jock Jams bumping (and if you have better taste in music, still avoid cranking the volume even though we all appreciate your sophisticated musical preference). In general, try your best to protect the nature experience that you're seeking yourself. Then you can sing "Kumbaya" and not feel like a hypocrite.

CHAPTER SIXTEEN

GAMES TO PLAY

When Heather was a child, her family spent a lot of time camping in various campgrounds around the United States. While she and her sister, Melissa, truly loved exploring the areas, she can now admit that their mother's background as a plant biologist was less than thrilling to her preteen daughters. Family hikes became nature walks as her mom tried to educate the girls on native plants and their usefulness to the Indigenous communities. As an almost forty-year-old woman, this stuff now fascinates Heather, but as a kid? *Forget about it.* Mom was boring.

Once, after a particularly long "nature walk" in Yellowstone National Park, Heather's family returned to their campsite to relax for the afternoon. Heather and Melissa, feeling a bit bored and looking for some excitement to liven up the day, invented a new game to play. To this day, neither woman remembers the real point of the game, but that definitely didn't matter. The object: Keep the car keys away from each other while their parents relaxed in the tent. As the eldest, Heather concocted a grand plan that would certainly elude her younger (and less intelligent, obvi) sister: Lock the keys in the car. How had Melissa not thought of this yet?! It was the perfect hiding spot!

It didn't take long for Heather to realize her superior plan was actually a terrible idea. She and Melissa huddled together in an effort to mastermind a recovery that avoided waking their parents with the truth. Fortunately, a solution to their plight hit the two of them like a bolt of lightning: Why not use a small tree branch to unlock the car door? Genius!

Until the twig snapped off in the lock. Of course.

Finally, dejected and fairly positive that their parents were going to disown them after abandoning them in Yellowstone forever, Heather and Melissa woke their mom and dad from their peaceful slumber and admitted the entire story. As one can imagine, it didn't go well.

But you know what did go well? Camping next door to an ex-convict with a background in lock picking. Who knew such a diverse range of talent was available at Yellowstone National Park?

We share this story for two reasons. First of all, don't trust your children. Ever. Second, this now absurdly hysterical story could have been avoided if Heather and Melissa had redirected their energy toward appropriate and probably more entertaining camp games. Lock picking is clearly the subpar choice when you have scavenger hunts and flashlight tag to enjoy, right?

We've rounded up some of our favorite camp games here. Many don't involve props or any type of prep work, meaning creativity is the only limit on where your game goes. Trust us: We've enjoyed some of these games for hours without ever growing bored!

NATURE SCAVENGER HUNT
POINT IT OUT!

PINECONE

BIRDS

CARDINAL :CHIRP:

Rat a TAT

:Peep:

Red-Bellied WOODPECKER *OR ANY WOODPECKER

:Peep:

:CHIRP:

BLUE JAY

BLACK-CAPPED CHICKADEE

WILD FLOWERS [COUNT THE DIFFERENT TYPES]

A REALLY ROUND ROCK (OR OTHER COOL SHAPES)

MUSHROOMS

Local ANIMAL PRINTS

DEER

OPOSSUM

T. Rex

ELK

RED FOX

FROG

LOCAL WILDLIFE

ON LAND

IN WATER

Ask a Ranger!

BUGS THAT FLY ----?---- **AND BUGS THAT DON'T...**

Bee

MONARCH

FIREFLY

LEAVES of DIFFERENT

SHAPES AND COLORS

TREE ROOTS

AN ADULT THAT NEEDS TO ACT LIKE A KID

FOSSILS

ACTIVE GAMES

Get the whole family moving (and maybe tired?) with games that involve lots of energy.

LIMBO

We've all played limbo at a birthday party, a roller-skating rink, or even at a bar when the clock struck twelve-thirty and the tequila came out (anyone?). But limbo also makes a great camp game, because it doesn't require any type of prep work and it is entertaining for a variety of ages. If you can find a dead branch on the ground, use that as your limbo stick. If not, use some string or even a hiking pole and create your obstacle. If you have music, all the better, but you may not need it, since there is a great chance that raucous laughter will fill the air anyway.

CAMPSITE OBSTACLE COURSE

We'll admit: We've been at campsites with grown-ass adults who created obstacle courses that lasted for hours. Was whiskey involved? Potentially, but that doesn't take away from the real-life fun factor. Everyone loves a good obstacle course because we can't resist the concept of beating the clock. You don't need to bring any props for this, either; use what you can find around camp. Picnic tables, camp chairs, coolers, and vehicles all make great features. Running, jumping, push-ups, and crawling seem to be popular activities to include too. Truly, the options are limitless.

NATURE SCAVENGER HUNT

If you are feeling like a super parent, you can prepare this game at home by printing out a list of items, including some special ones that you can secretly pack yourself. But if your organizational skills are more in line with Heather's and you don't remember this game until the exact moment your kid says, "I'm bored," it will still work. Come up with a list of fifteen to twenty items commonly found in nature, such as pinecones, birds, or wildflowers. Then pair up and head out together to locate and identify all the items on your list. Finding the objects is a lot of fun, but be sure to educate your children on why they should not take them. This creates a great opportunity to chat about Leave No Trace.

HIDE-AND-SEEK

It is an oldie but a goodie—and you can never go wrong with hide-and-seek. The premise is simple, but consider establishing a perimeter that contains the potential hiding spots. That way you don't need to worry about an embarrassing moment with the sheriff when you try to explain that your missing child was actually hiding behind a tree two miles away.

FLASHLIGHT TAG

As dusk falls, the flashlights and headlamps come out, opening up a new world of fun. This game is just like normal tag except only one person is wearing a headlamp or flashlight—he is the tagger. The others run all over trying to avoid being "hit" with his beam of light. Once a player is tagged, he is out until the next round.

GAMES THAT REQUIRE EQUIPMENT

These games required building or buying equipment, but they're a lot of fun whether you are camping in a national park or in your backyard.

BEANBAG TOSS / CORNHOLE

Depending on where you live, this game has a lot of different names: bags, cornhole, beanbags, bag chuck, or our personal favorite, hillbilly horseshoes. Regardless of what you call it, the premise is the same: Chuck some beanbags into some holes. You can build or buy the boards yourself, and all you need is a few holes cut into the boards. Teams line

up on opposites sides and take turns trying to throw the beanbags into the holes. The first team to get to twenty-one (or whatever number you decide is good for your group's attention span) wins.

LADDER TOSS

Like cornhole, this game involves throwing, but with a twist. The equipment needed is simple: one or two ladderlike structures and two sets of bolas, or strings with balls tied on each end. Once again, pair up in teams and take turns tossing the bolas toward the ladder, trying to get the strings to wrap around or otherwise stay on one of the rungs. Different rungs can equal a different number of points. If you feel like making the game spicier for older kids or adults, trying knocking bolas from the other team off the rungs. It isn't easy, but it heats up the competition in a hurry.

LIFE-SIZE JENGA

To be fair, it doesn't have to be the life-size version; you can play the standard game on a picnic table too. But the big version is just so much fun! Crafty types can easily build their own version of this game, but if you aren't the handy sort, don't stress; you can buy it in stores or online. The premise is the same as normal Jenga, only now the ground is your base and the tower gets to be as tall (or taller) than the people playing. Whoever pulls the plank that causes the tower to crash is the loser of the round.

TRASH-BAG SACK RACE

If you are feeling spicy, you can definitely sub in sleeping bags for this game, but that seems like a bad idea, unless you are angling for a way to justify the purchase of new sleeping bags. If that's the case, swap out the trash bags for your sleeping bags and let the destruction commence! Just like a traditional sack race, line everyone up in a trash bag and identify a finish line. Whoever hops the fastest, wins.

TENT GAMES

Sometimes bad weather happens to good people. If you are stuck in the tent for a few hours weathering out a storm, consider playing any of these games.

SHADOW PUPPETS

This typically works best with a younger crowd, although inebriated adults seem to think it's a good time too. Using a flashlight or headlamp, get creative with the types of shadow animals (or . . . creatures) you can create on the tent wall. For adults, we like to say that the most inappropriate shadow wins. Have at it.

MAD LIB STORYTIME

We love this game since it can work for a variety of ages (and a variety of maturity levels, if you know what we mean). One person starts the game by telling a story. After two or three sentences, he abruptly stops in the middle and passes the story to the next person, who continues where the first person left off. Continue this way until everyone has participated, and enjoy laughing as the plot takes all sorts of twists and turns.

THUMB (OR ARM) WRESTLING

We are going to leave it up to you to determine whether the thumb or the arm is the best option for your posse. Regardless, wrestling with any body parts tends to be fun for all ages. Move the sleeping pads and bags and create a ring in the middle to get this party started.

CHAPTER SEVENTEEN

TOP PLACES TO FRONTCOUNTRY CAMP

Now that you've got the gear and enough knowledge to keep you alive out there, it's time for the next big decision: Where do you want to camp? After all, you can't just pull up to any ol' patch of trees and pitch a tent; not only is that wicked boring, but it is likely illegal (in which case, don't call us). But with such a plethora of beautiful public lands at your fingertips, how do you decide which natural wonder to visit first?

We've got your back. With our combined years of expertise, we've scoured the country for our favorite camping areas. Some we love thanks to their unique nature and magnificent beauty, while others made the list simply because they have fewer bugs. Totally your call on which criteria are more important. Either way, this handy list means you have zero excuses; time to get off that couch and sleep in the dirt.

ACADIA NATIONAL PARK, MAINE

As the only national park in the entirety of New England (and the oldest park east of the Mississippi River), Acadia has a reputation to uphold. Thankfully, this park earns her stripes with grace. Campers looking for some amenities will love the three campgrounds: Blackwoods, Seawall, and Schoodic Woods. While you can't go wrong with any of them, we'd recommend Schoodic Woods. As the newest campground in the park, it feels much roomier and less cramped than the other two. The entire campground has ninety-four campsites (thirty for RVs), and each one has a picnic table and a fire ring. Washrooms with flush toilets and drinkable water are available too, meaning you can easily rehydrate yourself if you drink too much whiskey around the campfire.

BLACK HILLS NATIONAL FOREST, SOUTH DAKOTA

We'd make the argument that the Badlands are one of the most underrated gems of the National Park Service system. Not only does the park have one of the most complete sets of fossils ever discovered, but it's also a sweet stargazing spot. Annual astronomy events are held in the park for this very reason, so imagine how glorious it would be to watch meteors from the comfort of your tent.

But maybe you want to take a break from the structured campgrounds inside national parks? Totally get it. In that case, check out the nearby Black Hills National Forest. Dispersed camping is free and you can find

Black
Hills
National
Forest

90 MIN →

BADLANDS
NATIONAL PARK

40 MIN →

MOUNT RUSHMORE

30 MIN

CRAZY
HORSE
MEMORIAL

60 MIN

WIND CAVE
NATIONAL PARK

a private campsite nestled within the ponderosa pines. Plus, you're only a ninety-minute drive from Badlands National Park, sixty minutes from Wind Cave National Park, and a short hop, skip, and a step away from both Mount Rushmore and the Crazy Horse Memorial. Three cheers for proximity!

GRAND CANYON NATIONAL PARK, ARIZONA

There is no thrill better than sleeping on the rim of a big ditch, you know? That's why Grand Canyon National Park is a must-do no matter how many crowds of people descend upon this giant hole each year. Once there, you need to make a decision: North Rim or South Rim? The South Rim is warmer, more popular, and easily accessible, but the North Rim is peaceful and quiet, albeit a bit chilly. We've visited both numerous times and you really can't go wrong with either. If you visit in the summer, our pick is the Desert View Campground located twenty-five miles east of Grand Canyon Village on the South Rim. No reservations are needed; everything is first come, first served. There are no RV hookups, which makes for a quieter respite, but it is popular—the campground usually fills by noon each day, so get your butt in gear if you want a site.

CHANNEL ISLANDS NATIONAL PARK, CALIFORNIA

We'll admit: This is a questionable frontcountry categorization. But if you've ever wanted to camp on a remote island in the middle of the ocean, Channel Islands National Park is the place of your dreams. Located fifty miles off the coast of California, this grouping of five islands is a great way to combine the ease of frontcountry preparation with the self-reliant and isolated nature of the backcountry. Obviously, you can't drive here. Instead, campers and day-trippers alike catch a ferry from Ventura Harbor.

Each island has one established campground. For your first visit, we'd recommend Scorpion Canyon Campground on Santa Cruz Island. It's an easy and flat ten-minute walk from the boat harbor to the campground, so campers can bring wheeled duffels and even coolers if they want. Once there, it's about as peaceful as a campground can be. Pro tip: The wily foxes on the island have learned that the campground is a treasure trove of treats. No joke—they are smart little buggers. Stash all of your food in the included food storage box, and don't take your eyes off them for one second. True story: One distracted Heather by brushing against her feet while another snuck around from the back to snatch our bag of granola!

GREAT SMOKY MOUNTAINS NATIONAL PARK, TENNESSEE

Ol' Smoky is the most-visited park in the country for good reason. It's teeming with nature, wildlife, and waterfalls, but more notable is the history found within the park's confines (of course, it helps that it is smack dab next to so many people). More than seventy structures still exist, scattered throughout the park as leftover remnants from the prehistoric era. If you're into old stuff, you'll especially dig on the log buildings; it's the largest collection east of the Mississippi.

There are campgrounds aplenty, and each has running water and toilets for those who are disinclined to pee outside. Each of the ten campgrounds has a different personality, so it's best to find one that matches your style. Want to be near all the action? Then Cades Cove Campground is your best bet, as it's the most popular in the park.

ICEFIELDS PARKWAY, BANFF NATIONAL PARK, CANADA

The Icefields Parkway is a must-visit road trip for anyone who loves the outdoors, thanks to its rugged peaks, aqua-colored lakes, and proximity to gigantic wildlife, such as moose and grizzly bears. The Waterfowl Lakes Campground is located in the thick of things, just thirty-five miles north of Lake Louise. From June 22 through September 3, this isolated campground is available on a first-come, first-served basis. Cell phones don't work there, but who really cares when you have lakes out the front door that look like someone has dumped a box of crayons in the water.

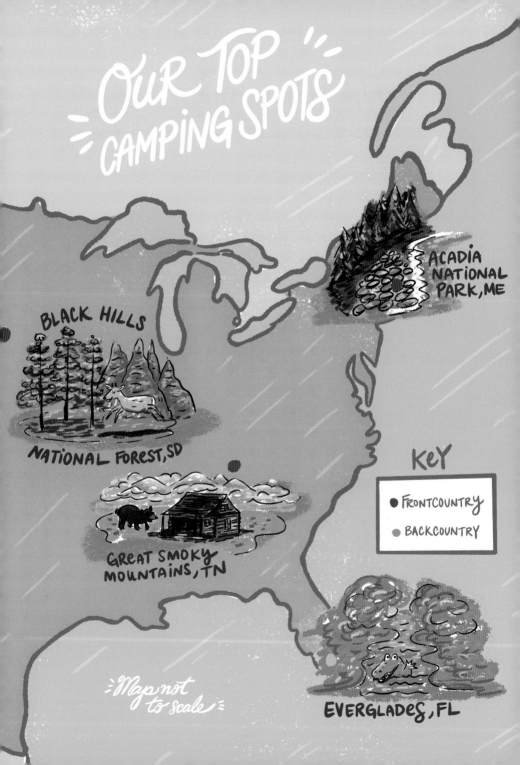

PACIFIC RIM NATIONAL PARK, BRITISH COLUMBIA, CANADA

Picture this: more than twelve miles of beautiful sand that stretches along the ocean, practically inviting visitors to scan the horizon in search of great whales. Perched on a ledge above Long Beach sits Green Point Campground, the only campground on the entire swath of sand. Campsites are close enough to the beach that the sound of ocean waves lulls everyone to sleep. Glorious.

CHAPTER EIGHTEEN

ROAD TRIPS

When we found out we were expecting our daughter, we made the decision to capitalize

on Will's paternity leave (he could take it anytime before she turned one) with an alternative form of family hazing: a three-month camping road trip through the American West. As if learning how to operate on minimal sleep while a tiny dictator ran the show wasn't enough to throw our world into a spiral, we opted to add tents and sleeping bags into the mix. As two adults, we'd completed many road trips together, but the prep work was minimal. After all, slapping a sleeping bag in the dirt and eating a granola bar works fine if you're a grown-ass adult and understand your situation (and meal choice) is temporary. That isn't the case when you have a seven-month-old baby girl in tow who wants nothing other than a boob or a bottle and cannot fathom why Mom is slathering sunscreen all over her cheeks every five minutes. My friends, the learning curve was steep.

But you know what? We survived, and dare we say thrived? We'll just go ahead and say that. To this day, we both reflect on that twelve-week adventure with nothing but the goofiest of grins on our faces. Sure, we experienced a few bumps and bruises along the way as we navigated the dos and don'ts of a family camping road trip, but we regret nothing and learned everything. (For example: A Pack 'n Play parked under a tree in the middle-of-nowhere Utah does not make for an infant-approved bed, since she will likely find the chirping birds and blowing pine needles far more enjoyable than sleeping. Who knew?)

In all seriousness, we did glean some useful information that we are happy to pass on to others who wish to embark upon a camping road trip. It can be five days or five weeks long; it doesn't matter. All that matters is you create happy memories while learning to live out of the back of your vehicle.

SEVEN TIPS FOR A CAMPING ROAD TRIP

GOOGLE MAPS IS A FICKLE FRIEND

It's the twenty-first century: Let's stop pretending that we still use paper maps for auto navigation. Okay?

In this modern era, it is easy to rely on Google Maps (or whatever navigational app you prefer) for any and all directions. But that Google, she can be fickle as she lures you into a sense of false confidence in your navigational abilities. If the GPS tells you that your next location is five hours away, plan for just a bit more, and don't forget to leave early. There is nothing worse than showing up after dark and pitching your tent on a cactus because you didn't allot enough time for the journey.

COME UP WITH AN ORGANIZATIONAL SYSTEM

Remember the game Tetris? If you're good at Tetris, you'll be a pro at the logistics that come with a camping road trip. It doesn't matter if you're traveling in a truck or a car; it will likely be packed to the brim with equipment. Find a system that works for you and stick with it. For us, we opted for large plastic bins to contain like gear with like gear. Each container always went back in the exact same location and each item stored in the exact same bin. That way, you always know where your headlamp or camp shoes are without a lot of frustration and rummaging.

LIVE LARGE IN A SPACIOUS TENT

We're all about ultralight gear when we're backpacking, but a camping road trip is not the place to scrimp on livability. Since you do not need to carry the weight or the size, opt up and bring a tent that is more spacious than you actually need. For two adults and an infant, we brought a four-person tent, and it was perfect: We shared half, our nine-pound wonder took over the other half. Large vestibules can be nice in case you're stuck waiting out a storm inside, but certainly make sure you have extra

LEVEL 4
SCORE 1526

room for gear so you don't have to constantly run back and forth to your vehicle every time you forget an item.

PACK A QUALITY COOLER

These may be fighting words, but there is a good chance our massive Otterbox cooler was our favorite item on the whole trip. Not only did it work exceedingly well, but we used it just like a portable fridge. We kept it inside our truck's cab while driving so Heather could reach over and make healthy snacks for the family during long-haul days. At camp, it became an outdoor refrigerator as well as an impromptu table or seat, depending on what we needed most. It worked so well that we could even stash our daughter's breast milk inside without fear of spoiling. If you decide to invest, nab a cooler that includes a shelf for items to sit above the ice. This keeps cheeses and chocolate bars from turning into a waterlogged, unpalatable mess.

DON'T FORGET A CAMP STOVE

It is beyond easy to eat a crapload of junk food on road trips, especially when your only options are McDonald's or the local gas station. But if you pack a camp stove, you don't have to rely on made-for-you foods, and you will save a ton of money in the process. Besides, is there a greater joy than rolling over in the morning and drinking a cup of piping-hot coffee while watching the sun rise? We think not.

DON'T BE A DIRTBAG – WASH YO' FACE

We get it: It's fine to be dirty, and there is no better time to live in your own stench than while camping. But if you are doing a long-term camping road trip, you need to shower at some point, or at least wipe off visible dirt so people *think* you've showered. For us, we have two options. The first and easiest is baby wipes. We used these even before we had a baby, which is excellent, because now there is a bonus stash lying around all the time. Baby wipes are soft and gentle (find wipes that use natural fibers like bamboo pulp or wood rather than plastic and polyester to help out the environment), yet they clean the majority of dirt off your face and nether regions so you won't stink to the high heavens when you're in public places, like gas stations. But if you've been on the road for a minute and you're so far gone that even the wildlife smells you from twenty miles away, consider a camp shower. Ours holds three gallons of water and pressurizes with a small foot pump so you don't need gravity for it to work its magic. Plus, it does a great job of cleaning out diaper blowouts . . . just don't ask us how we know.

DON'T BE AFRAID TO LIVE IN THE LAP OF LUXURY

Depending on how long you're traveling, don't be afraid to fork over some cash on occasion and splurge on a hotel room. During our twelve weeks of road tripping, our longest stretch of tent life was twelve nights. Yes, we were ripe at that point! We nabbed a cheap hotel room and quickly realized that a single night of hot water and seventeen pillows could reorient our brains in a positive way. After that point, we opted for one hotel per week, and we're still convinced it was the best game-time decision we made.

ROAD TRIP ESSENTIALS

SPACIOUS ∴TENT∴

"QUALITY COOLER"

∴CAMP STOVE∴

STAY CLEAN!

CHAPTER NINETEEN

CONCLUSION

We once read a meme that described camping as the art of getting closer to nature while getting farther from a cold beverage and a hot shower. It is accurate, but it also misses the point. To us, the best memories are made camping (and it is certainly cheaper than therapy).

Time in Mother Nature is always time well spent, regardless of whether you enjoy your first camping trip with your mother, brother, significant other, or oddly lovable mailman who happened to swing by when you were packing the car. You can stress over the gear and the logistics as much as you want, but in the end, camping is all about the stories you create with the people who come along for the ride. Just make sure to log that shower when you get home. You don't want to be *that person* in someone else's story.

ACKNOWLEDGMENTS

I love surprises, and no surprise brings me greater joy than when I have the opportunity to surprise my wife. Despite legitimate warnings from our publisher, we opted to coauthor this book, and the final text is something that makes me extremely proud. The pride doesn't come from the words we wrote—rather it comes from how I feel after getting a front-row seat to what it's like to work with an author as brilliant as Heather. As a young girl she knew she wanted to be a writer—seriously, how many people can say they're fulfilling their childhood professional dream?!—and now she's doing it, and she's damn good at it, too.

So, to the surprise: Sweetheart, you have no idea this is going to be in the book and you're probably going to kill me when you read it, but I want you to know how grateful I am to be yours. You are an inspiration to me and the perfect role model for our daughter, who I know will also be inspired by the woman you are. You have my best, always.

I would also like to thank our illustrator, Laura Fisk. You've given this book character and color that separate it from an everyday text into something bright, entertaining, and the kind of thing I'm excited to show our kid as soon as she's old enough to stop ripping pages out of books because she likes a picture. Working with you has been nothing but fun, and with a little luck this won't be the last time.

Finally, I would like to thank our editor, Lisa White. I feel so very fortunate you chose to work with us, and over the past months you've shown why you are a consummate professional in your field. Thank you for knowing when to tolerate our peculiar vernacular and obscure pop-culture references, and when to rein them in because not even the most-seasoned *Gilmore Girls* aficionado would have a clue as to what something meant. Working with you to bring this book to life has been a dream come true, and I'll never forget everything you've done to help us get here.

With immense gratitude, Will

INDEX